HOW TO KEEP YOUR JOY

HOW TO KEEP YOUR JOY

PAUL WALKER

OLIVER
NELSON

A Division of Thomas Nelson Publishers
Nashville • Atlanta • Camden • New York

Published in Nashville, Tennessee, by Oliver-Nelson Books,
a division of Thomas Nelson, Inc., Publishers, and
distributed in Canada by Lawson Falle, Ltd., Cambridge,
Ontario.

Unless otherwise noted, the Bible version used in this
publication is THE NEW KING JAMES VERSION.
Copyright © 1979, 1980, 1982, Thomas Nelson, Inc.,
Publishers.

Scripture quotations noted NIV are taken from the HOLY
BIBLE: NEW INTERNATIONAL VERSION. Copyright
© 1973, 1978, 1984 by the International Bible Society. Used
by permission of Zondervan Bible Publishers.

Scripture quotations noted PHILLIPS are from J. B. Phillips:
THE NEW TESTAMENT IN MODERN ENGLISH,
Revised Edition. © J. B. Phillips 1958, 1960, 1972. Used
by permission of Macmillan Publishing Co., Inc.

Scripture quotations noted TLB are taken from *The Living
Bible,* copyright 1971 by Tyndale House Publishers,
Wheaton, IL. Used by permission.

The extract from "Stress: A Sure Prescription" on pp. 126,
127 is reprinted with permission NEW WOMAN
MAGAZINE and THE TIMES OF LONDON
SYNDICATE.

Names, circumstances, and letters have been fictionalized for
protection of privacy.

Printed in the United States.

Library of Congress Cataloging-in-Publication Data

Walker, Paul L.
  How to keep your joy.

  Bibliography: p.
  1. Christian life—Church of God authors.
I. Title.
BV4501.2.W3223 1987   248.4'899   86-33170
ISBN 0-8407-9076-7

1 2 3 4 5 6 — 92 91 90 89 88 87

To the memory of A. V. (Gus) Howell,
pastor—friend—father-in-law,
a man whose lifetime as a pastor
symbolized the meaning of joy.

CONTENTS

ACKNOWLEDGMENTS

In a day when the number one buzzword is stress, successful living is dependent upon our development of the emotional and spiritual resources of biblical joy.

With this premise in mind, the purpose of this book is to chart a course for maintaining a sense of inner gladness as an abiding strength for troublesome times.

The material in these chapters has been compiled from life experiences as a pastor as translated into sermons delivered to the Mount Paran congregation. I am personally indebted to this family of believers for their enthusiastic support, involved interest, and dedicated discipleship. It is through our shared experiences that these concepts of joy have emerged.

Many people have been involved in bringing this project to completion. My personal gratitude is extended to my wife, Carmelita, for her constant encouragement; to Donna Cutbirth, my administrative assistant, for her insight and suggestions; to Susan Dotson, for her research and typing of the finished manuscript; and to the pastoral staff, administrative staff, lay leadership, and congregation of the Mount Paran Church of God, for their cooperation and involvement in "hammering out" the joy sustainers herein presented.

Paul Walker, Ph.D.
Senior Pastor
Mount Paran Church of God
Atlanta, Georgia

1 *Stress Point*

Sense of Inadequacy

DISCOVERING WHAT JOY IS

Scriptural
Source

Philippians 4:1–8

Joy
Sustainers

Embrace a spiritual stance
Embrace a security source
Embrace a soaring style

1

DISCOVERING WHAT JOY IS

It was 6:30 A.M. I had just come down for breakfast when the telephone rang. My mother answered it, turned pale, and called for me. In trembling words she said, "Your father has been in a terrible accident. He is in the Raleigh General Hospital [Beckley, West Virginia] in critical condition. He may not survive."

My father, Paul H. Walker, a minister for over thirty years at the time, was chairman of the World Missions Board for the Church of God. He and a visiting minister from overseas had been driving home together when the accident occurred. Traveling late at night in the fog and rain, my father had come around a West Virginia hairpin curve and broadsided a locomotive parked across the road while coal cars were being loaded. My father and his friend were severely injured, and my father's life was in jeopardy because of extensive internal injuries.

After being briefed by the doctor, my mother and I went into the hospital room to see my father. My mother took his hands in hers and asked, "Paul, how do you feel?"

As a questioning teenager concerned about the meaning of life, the best route for happiness and success, and the legitimacy of the Christian faith, I wondered how he would answer. In my mind, my mother's question was the acid test of his Christian witness. His answer would prove his true beliefs.

Does faith work in crises? Are there sufficient resources in Christ to meet the bad times? Can we cope with tragedy and still be happy? Is there such a thing as joy in the midst of trouble? These haunting thoughts ran through my mind.

My father's answer, and his firm faith in the healing process, changed my life perspective. With his head swollen twice its normal size, his rib cage, breastbone, kneecap, and kneebone shattered, and his legs broken, he made a single statement of joy: "I feel terrible pain in my body, but I am happy in my soul and spirit."

As a somewhat cynical youth, I thought, *How can this possibly be? How is it possible to say such a thing in such a miserable condition— terrible in body, happy in soul?* It seemed to be the contradiction of all contradictions.

But as I thought about this situation, I suddenly received new insight into the meaning of the word *joy.* I had sung about it, read about it, heard my father preach about it all my life. But there it was before me in living reality.

In my father's words:

> While I was sitting on the bench in the rain waiting for the ambulance, at the place of the wreck, I prayed and told the Lord I was ready to go, but that I had preached for Him over thirty years and that I would like to live and raise my family, if He would let me. Just then a bright and glorious light came, the same in appearance that I had seen at my conversion, only much larger. A great warmth of consolation came over me and I had the assurance that my life would be spared.[1]

It was as though this event brought closure to my understanding of the meaning of faith and the process of happiness. I came to understand a tough-minded approach to Christian living that maintains joy regardless of the circumstances.

My father died in 1975, twenty-six years after the accident, but the impact of that experience—having occurred at a critical time in my life—ignited an intense desire for the Christian life motivated through the power of spiritual joy.

From that time on, I adopted the words of the apostle Paul as my theme for living: "I always pray with joy. . . . [I] rejoice with all of you. . . . Rejoice in the Lord always. I will say it again: Rejoice!" (Phil. 1:4; 2:17; 4:4 NIV).

What a fantastic outlook! The apostle Paul learned how to live the life of joy—regardless (see Phil. 4:11–13).

In Acts 21 Paul was bound in chains and taken to a Jerusalem jail because of his witness of the faith. In Acts 23 he was spirited away at night and taken to Caesarea by the Sea by two hundred soldiers, seventy horsemen, and two hundred spearmen to protect him from a threatened attack by his enemies. In Acts 24 he was caught in a political bribes game and languished in a Caesarean prison for two years. In Acts 6 he appealed to Caesar on the basis of his Roman citizenship and was shipped off to Rome.

From approximately A.D. 61 to 63 he was confined in Caesar's custody and chained daily to a palace guard. From about A.D. 63 to 64 he was released for a short period of time. From about A.D. 64 to 68 he was reincarcerated and probably confined to the Mamertine Prison in Rome—no windows, no bed, no table or chairs—a deep underground stone cave with only a small opening in the ceiling for contact with the outside world. Finally, in about A.D. 68, he was beheaded on Nero's chopping block.

For ten years it was as though a Damoclean sword hung over his head. What was his response? Paul wrote a letter to a band of believers in Philippi and told them eleven times to rejoice and five times to have joy.

HANDLING THE HORIZONTAL

Keeping Paul's advice in mind, we need to think about how we have joy. How do we handle joy on the horizontal, or secular, plane? What is the human approach?

To many people, joy is a *good feeling*—a sense of what we call happiness.

To others, joy is a *sense of adjustment*—a set of workable response patterns derived from a realistic understanding of ourselves. Joy is becoming mature and learning by experience. It is a sense of independence that enables us to make decisions and act upon them appropriately. It is the ability to generate and control the good things in life rather than be pawns of others.

Many human ways are available for finding the good life embodied in the concept of joy. If we feel better, become better adjusted, and learn how to help ourselves live a more effective life, it is true that we will be more efficient in maintaining our sense of joy. It is possible to laugh our way to health under the right circumstances. We can release our inner selves and relate better to others and the world around us by loving ourselves appropriately. If we have faith in ourselves and embrace positive attitudes and creative energies, we can overcome fear and develop a sense of confidence.

If horizontal joy is all we have, however, we may find ourselves in the position of that haunting pop tune made famous by Peggy Lee, "Is That All There Is?"

EXPERIENCING THE VERTICAL

Happiness on the horizontal plane alone is a tenuous balance between what we think we ought to get out of life and what we really get. For most people, happiness or joy in the secular sense boils down to the way in which we handle our circumstances rather than to the severity of the circumstances themselves.

It is easier for us to be happy if we are educated and are financially secure, but all is in vain if we are working too much, battling stress, and experiencing a lousy home life. It is easier to be happy if we are married to persons we love, but if spouses never see each other and live as prisoners of loneliness, what difference does love make?

Joy at its highest meaning calls for the vertical, or spiritual, dimension that translates superficial happiness, productive adjustment, and self-help techniques into an encounter with God. Joy becomes the power of God's grace, the process of God's spirit, and the presence of God's nature in our lives.

In the biblical sense, joy then becomes a spiritual balance between expectations and achievements—the ability to approach problems objectively by accepting things as they are and working toward solution and adjustment. Assuming this stance, joy is a sense of imperturbable gladness that sings when rejected, praises when persecuted, and stands when attacked. (See Acts 16:25; Acts 5:41; 2 Chron. 20:14–30.) *v. 20 . . . put your trust in the Lord your God, and you will be established.*

In this sense, joy is taking our crises in stride and utilizing our *Put your trust in his prophets if you will succeed* circumstances to bring glory to God. It is seeking first the kingdom of God and His righteousness. It is knowing full well that all things we need—and can realistically handle—will be given to us as we live secure in the knowledge that God loves us.

JOY IS A SPIRITUAL STANCE

The joy that I'm describing is what the apostle Paul had in mind when he told the Philippians to "stand fast in the Lord"

(Phil. 4:1). Paul could tell them to rejoice in the Lord and find joy in Him because he had learned to stand fast in the Lord and have joy. The Greek word used is *stēko,* and it carries the connotation of standing upright in spite of surrounding circumstances. As Kittel puts it,

> In faith man attains to the position which allows him to stand firm. This standing does not result from secular security such as health, power, property or connections. It is based on the transcendent God on whose promise faith is fixed. It is here the human existence finds its foundation and establishment.[2]

Taking a firm spiritual stance is the meaning of joy, and it is vividly illustrated in a death crisis experienced by the Thomas family. Bob died unexpectedly in a head-on collision the evening before he and his family—his wife, Carol, and son, Craig—were to join the church choir for a special Christmas concert in our nation's capital before a national television audience. It was the trip of a lifetime.

Such a sudden death for a well-respected Christian was a tragic blow to the entire church, but in this case it had special significance. Craig was the featured soloist and could scarcely be replaced at such a late date.

What do you do when tragedy strikes as you are packing to take a family trip that has been a lifelong dream?

You stand firm!

Carol and Craig remained behind one day, attended the funeral and the interment, and then joined the group in Washington and finished the tour as a part of the ministry. Sure they were crushed. Sure they grieved. Sure they felt the loss and emptiness of death. But they *also found joy* by standing firm.

To use Carol's words:

> The way God's love comes through others amazes me. From the night of Bob's death until this very day, I have not felt alone. Maybe briefly, but not for very long. God, through someone or something, shows me His love.
>
> Let me share this with you. Sometime after we arrived in Washington, I woke one morning with the song "Whispering Hope" on my mind. I sang it. Then, for about three days that song kept going through my mind. . . . I would say to Craig, "It's still there—I still hear it." Isn't our Lord precious?
>
> The trip was certainly the right thing for us. Leaving here wasn't easy, but we felt the Lord was in this thing from the very beginning. Now, in retrospect, we know it was all in His plan.
>
> Yes, we still hurt, but there will be a way. This same God that's been so near won't leave us now. There are many things to do, but I am taking them one by one and trusting the Lord to lead me the right way.

This is the way to begin to discover joy—to take a spiritual stance.

JOY IS A SECURITY SOURCE

Paul took it a step further, however, and boldly affirmed that we are to "be anxious for nothing." In fact, he said, "In everything by prayer and supplication, with thanksgiving, let your requests be made known to God; and the peace of God, which surpasses all understanding, will guard your hearts and minds through Christ Jesus" (Phil. 4:6,7).

Here, in just a few short sentences, we find the very source of joy—the security of knowing that God cares, God listens, God gives peace.

Making it work, however, is sometimes easier said than done. Be anxious for nothing? Sounds impossible! After all, we are conditioned by the things that happen around us, and the way we respond often determines the status of our joy.

That's why we need the response of faith. Joy, then, becomes the response of faith in the Father as our security source.

A teenager named Susan is practicing this joy. Although she is only sixteen years old, she is battling lymphoma—a dreaded cancer that attacks the lymph glands. For the past few years she has been undergoing rigorous chemotherapy, but she "hangs in tough" and plays first base for a school-sponsored softball team. A letter from her mother shares some details of her story:

> Three years ago, a young girl placed a note in the collection plate of her church. The note was from my daughter, and it went something like this:
>
> "Dear pastor, I am thirteen years old, my name is Susan, and I have cancer. Please pray for me."
>
> In the months and then years that followed, I have watched Susan's inner spirit blossom. And I've seen how her expectant disposition has affected the lives of all those with whom she comes into contact. Because Susan's faith is firmly rooted in Jesus, she has been able to overcome her own sense of fear and has been able to pass along her joy to other teenage cancer patients. Susan's spiritual understanding far surpasses her youth. With so much negativity around us, it is wonderful to see Susan use her situation to help others know the peace of God.

In describing another young cancer patient, writer Salynn Boyles reflected his feelings in a most stirring editorial:

> It is obvious in listening to Jason talk about his disease that Jason has accepted it with the maturity and understanding that are rare in anyone, regardless of age. He has remained optimistic throughout the ordeal, he says, due to his faith in God.
>
> "I am a Christian," he says. "I think Jesus is allowing this to

happen to prepare me for something so that later on in life I will
do something for Him."[3]

Perhaps this is what Christ meant when He told us that unless
we become as little children we cannot enter into the kingdom of
heaven (see Matt. 18:1–5). Somehow little children have a way of
coming to God and trusting Him with joy as their security
source.

JOY IS A SOARING STYLE

One of my recreational loves is downhill skiing. In the early
days of learning this sport, I took some lessons, and I remember
the instructor saying that I needed to think about *soaring* down
the mountain. I needed to relax, enjoy riding the skis, and soar
down the mountain like I was riding on gelatin and carrying a
tray of expensive crystal I could not afford to break.

Somehow, this makes what Paul said in Philippians 4:8,9
mean more to me personally. In his own way he conveyed the
idea that joy comes when we learn to live the soaring style:

> Whatever things are true, whatever things are noble, whatever
> things are just, whatever things are pure, whatever things are
> lovely, whatever things are of good report, if there is any virtue
> and if there is anything praiseworthy—meditate on these
> things. The things which you learned and received and heard
> and saw in me, these do, and the God of peace will be with you.

This brings up the whole realm of attitudes, and in the words
of Thorndike and Hagin, "attitudes relate to tendencies to accept
or reject particular groups of individuals, sets of ideas, or social
institutions."[4]

Attitudes play a major role in the development of character, temperament, adjustment, and interest. In fact, attitudes shape our patterns of response and behavior in practically every phase of our lives.

Perhaps this explains why Paul was so concerned about the Philippians learning to rejoice in every situation. According to Philippians 4:2,3, two women, Euodia and Syntyche, were having problems and quarreling with each other. While we do not know the nature of their dispute, we do know that Paul called for a change in their attitudes, "to be of the same mind in the Lord" (Phil. 4:2). In fact, he called upon the entire church to develop a soaring style and help mend the breach.

In a contemporary sense this is what Felicia Lee is reporting in an article entitled "Cynical Attitude Harms Health." Basing her findings on a study done at Duke University, she concludes that "men who are cynical and hostile are more prone to heart disease and die earlier. . . . the results are further evidence that a negative state of mind may be hazardous to your health."[5]

There is no doubt about it. The Bible calls for a soaring style based upon a thought process of "whatever things are true . . . noble . . . just . . . pure . . . lovely . . . of good report . . . praiseworthy" (Phil. 4:8).

This is the meaning of joy—a soaring style based on a positive attitude.

A man named Martin found this to be true while battling inoperable cancer. Here is his story:

> I am free, free, free! Free in spirit, free in mind, free in expression. Nothing in the outer world can bind me or limit me. I am free from care, free to be happy, free to be loving and sharing today, free to be what God created me to be. . . .
> Jesus has showed me the why of suffering. I've found out that the person who must endure suffering will benefit from it if he is attentive to what the Lord is saying to him. As I look back over my life, I can personally testify that I could easily have done

without many joyful experiences, but I could not have spared one valuable spiritual lesson I have learned from sorrow! Why? Because, "God whispers in our pleasures but shouts in our pain!" The Lord forces us by our distresses to pay attention to His voice.

While such times of testing are not pleasant to endure, we must wait patiently for Him to accomplish His wise purposes. If we avoid becoming bitter in our earthly trials, we will learn the lessons of grace which only adversity can bring to the teachable heart. Those who accept troubles graciously grow rich by their losses, rise by their falls, and find new life in Christ by dying to self.

Often when God brings pressure into our lives, His purpose is to give us more power.

Discovering what joy is gives us a starting place for learning how to keep our joy. It is not enough to feel good about ourselves or to have positive attitudes, in spite of our circumstances; we need to stand fast in the Lord and find joy through Him. When we do this, we will be well on our way to having the soaring style of life He means for us to have, and we will gain a true sense of adequacy.

John 3:36 – He who believes in the Son has eternal life; but he who does not obey the Son shall not see life, but the wrath of God abides on Him.

Luke 12:43 – Blessed is that slave whom his master finds so doing when he comes.

John 15:05 – I am the vine, you are the branches; he who abides in me, and I in him, he bears much fruit, for apart from me you can do nothing.

John 15:15 – No longer do I call you slaves, for the slave does not know what his master is doing; but I have called you friends, for all things that I have heard from my father I have made known to you.

2

Stress Point

Lack of Meaning

DECIDING YOUR DISCIPLESHIP

Scriptural Sources

John 3:36

Luke 12:43

John 15:5

John 15:15

Acts 22:15

1 Peter 4:10

Matthew 5:14–16 – You are the light of the world. A city set on a hill cannot be hidden. Nor do men light a lamp and put it under a peck-measure, but on the lampstand and it gives light to all who are in the house. Let your light shine before men in such a way that they may see your good works, and glorify your father who is in heaven.

Joy Sustainers

Become a believer in faith

Become a servant in responsibility

Become a branch in union

Become a friend in privilege

Become a witness in testimony

Become a steward in trust

Become a light in influence

Acts 22:15 – For you will be a witness for Him to all men of what you have seen & heard.

I Peter 4:10 – As each one has received a special gift, employ it in serving one another, as good stewards of the manifold grace of God.

2

DECIDING YOUR DISCIPLESHIP

In the 1960s, a certain placard appeared at many protest rallies and social action marches. On this placard was the statement JESUS—YES! CHRISTIANITY—NO!

When we analyze the meaning of this statement, we realize that most of us have a real desire to know Christ and to experience His personhood, His power, and His presence. Yet it may be difficult to know Him fully because of all the differing interpretations, the insurmountable structures, the antiquated bureaucracy, and the traditions of institutionalism that surround Him. The beliefs advocated by these voices of authority often obscure Him from view and, in some instances, obliterate Him completely.

This came home hard to me during my seminary days as a systematic theology major. Although I really enjoyed the intellectual pursuit of philosophical insight and abstract constructs, it occurred to me that I had a *so what?* attitude. What value is doctrinal jargon if we don't know Him? if we don't know His person? if we don't experience His power? if we don't practice His presence? if we don't express His kingdom in our daily living? if we don't really have His joy?

Of the world's 4,781 billion people, some 1,548 billion profess to be Christian.[1] What do these statistics mean? The New Testament only uses the word *Christian* twice, whereas it uses the word *disciple* over three hundred times. But the word *Christian* has become such an overused, generalized, watered-down concept that it has little significance when reviewed in its original New Testament sense.

The New Testament church had joy because it captured the meaning of discipleship. This joy is expressed in Acts 2:46,47:

> So continuing daily with one accord in the temple, and breaking bread from house to house, they ate their food with gladness and simplicity of heart, praising God and having favor with all the people. And the Lord added daily those who were being saved.

In the New Testament sense, disciples are learners—followers of Jesus Christ in attitudes, beliefs, and values. Disciples are those who accept Christ as Messiah, submit to Him as Lord, and open their lives to the power of the Holy Spirit. Disciples are those who crucify the flesh, subdue traditions under the leadership of Christ, and regulate their lifestyles under the providence of God as revealed in the living Word of God. To keep joy, then, is (1) to make a lifestyle decision to be a disciple of Jesus Christ, (2) to live by the assurance that His power is adequate to overcome every obstacle, (3) to accept fully His call to follow Him, and (4) to utilize our best talents truly to become "fishers of men" (see Matt. 4:19; 8:22; Mark 1:17).

Those who keep their joy translate discipleship into kingdom living by recognizing that the kingdom of God is an *inner* life (see Luke 17:21), a *coping* life (see Heb. 12:28), a *persevering* life (see Luke 9:62; Acts 14:22), a *serving* life (see Matt. 5:3; 25:34,35), and an *inheritance* life (see James 2:5).

Discipleship living is kingdom living, and kingdom living is joyful living:

> For the kingdom of God is not eating and drinking, but righteousness and peace and joy in the Holy Spirit. For he who

serves Christ in these things is acceptable to God and approved by men (Rom. 14:17,18).

How, then, does a disciple live? What are the dimensions of discipleship that ensure our joy?

A BELIEVER IN FAITH

He who believes in the Son has everlasting life; and he who does not believe in the Son shall not see life, but the wrath of God abides on him (John 3:36).

First, a disciple is a *believer in faith.* The Greek word used in this passage of Scripture is *pistĕuō,* and it denotes a conviction motivated by our highest aspirations. A believer, then, experiences a joyful trust in Jesus as Lord and places full confidence in the ministry of God's messenger and His words. In this sense, we maintain our joy as we accept Christ at His word and emulate His lifestyle in every situation (see Phil. 4:11–13).

This is the experience of Connie, a physically abused runaway who was scared, angry, and confused. But she became a believer in faith. In her words:

I wanted desperately to be free. Totally free! Day after day my regret and grief became heavier and heavier in the chains I was carrying around! Struggling under such heavy chains caused bruise after bruise, pain upon pain, and scars that could not heal. This continued until I was unrecognizable, distorted, and mutilated beyond hope—hope—there's that word again that keeps haunting me! Who am I running from and why am I so afraid? . . . It was then that the Lord spoke to my heart and asked me when I was going to stop running in the opposite direction of His love, mercy, and grace. It was then that I found myself crawling to Him bringing to Him everything— surrendering all—the ugliness, the sin, the regret, the failure—

completely letting go. Little by little I opened my heart and hands and allowed Him to take all that hindered. . . . As I surrendered, "Guess what?" My heavenly Father exchanged all I gave Him for what I had prayed these past several years . . . healing and wholeness! . . . This wholeness and healing has transformed my life in ways I cannot express. I am a new creation, and I am loving every moment of it.

Connie became a believer in faith. She put her faith in Jesus Christ, and He sustained her with His life.

A SERVANT IN RESPONSIBILITY

Blessed is that servant whom his master will find so doing when he comes (Luke 12:43).

Second, a disciple is a *servant in responsibility*. The Greek word used here in this parable of stewardship and readiness is *döulŏs*, and it means literally "to be a slave." In the broadest sense, a servant gives his personhood wholly to another and gives total service for Christ in the kingdom of God. A servant yields to the will of God with disregard for selfish interest.

Accepting servanthood is accepting the fact that we are not our own. We were bought at a price. As Paul put it, "Do you not know that your body is a temple of the Holy Spirit who is in you, whom you have from God? . . . therefore, glorify God in your body" (1 Cor. 6:19,20).

Perhaps the concept of Christian servanthood can be illustrated by this story. Just before the Emancipation Proclamation was issued, a beautiful young black girl was separated from her family and put on the auction block. Motivated by lust and lewdness, the slave owners began to bid, but one bidder continually raised the call until all others had dropped out. Upon purchasing the girl, he surprised onlookers by writing her a certificate of freedom. He delivered her from slavery forever.

In an unprecedented act of gratitude, the girl ran after him, fell at his feet, and cried out in a loud voice, "Since you care enough for me to free me, it will be my highest honor to commit my life to you as a servant."

Servanthood is not coerced; it is not legislated; it is not mandated against the will. Rather, servanthood is chosen; it is sought; it is experienced in the transactions of Calvary that set us free to serve in joy.

A BRANCH IN UNION

I am the vine, you are the branches. He who abides in Me,
and I in him, bears much fruit; for without Me
you can do nothing (John 15:5).

Third, a disciple is a *branch in union*. The Greek word for branch is *klēma*, and it refers to a flexible, tender offshoot. A branch is of the same substance as the vine and survives by being sustained by the power of the vine.

In this sense we identify with Christ. A paradox becomes apparent when we call the roll, for it is a most unlikely crew of people who make up His disciples. We have to wonder at some of the choices.

As Bill Leonard stated:

It seems that the more I read the Scriptures, the more I think that this life we call the gospel is often held together for us by nothing but a bunch of clowns, the most surprising and foolish looking individuals that God or anybody else could find.[2]

Well, what about Noah? Noah was a silly old man who built an ark despite the fact that it had never rained—and he had the

31

audacity to say that God told him to build it. What about David? David was a smart kid with five stones who took on a giant twice his size. And then what about Simon Peter who played both sides against the middle? At Caesarea he called Jesus the Son of the living God, but in Jerusalem he claimed he never knew Him.

And what about us? He came to us and took us in when we were nothing. The apostle Peter said, "Once [you] were not a people but are now the people of God, who had not obtained mercy but now have obtained mercy" (1 Pet. 2:10). We are a chosen people, a royal priesthood, a holy nation—a people belonging to God. This means that we have been given a new status whereby we are called "to proclaim the praises of Him who called [us] out of darkness into His marvelous light" (1 Pet. 2:9).

This is how we keep our joy: We live as branches in union with Christ, who is the true vine and from whom we draw our strength.

A FRIEND IN PRIVILEGE

No longer do I call you servants, for a servant does not know
what his master is doing; but I have called you friends,
for all things that I heard from My Father
I have made known to you (John 15:15).

Fourth, a disciple is a *friend in privilege*. In this passage of Scripture the Greek word is *philös,* and it refers to the kind of friendship that is originated in faith, initiated by choice, and characterized by emotion.

The verb form implies the sense of affection we feel for a brother, a sister, or a close friend. In our relationship to Christ, however, the word takes on greater significance because He calls us not only friends but also heirs. In fact, the apostle Paul said we are "heirs of God and joint heirs with Christ" (Rom. 8:17). Jesus Himself said that on the day He judges the earth, He will say to those on His right hand to come and "inherit the kingdom prepared for you from the foundation of the earth" (Matt. 25:34).

John Tauler, a fourteenth-century mystic, illustrated this by telling a story of his chance meeting with a beggar on the street. In goodwill John said to him, "Hello, my friend, I hope that you have a very good day."

To his surprise, the beggar replied, "Every day for me is a good day."

In response John said, "Well, my friend, I hope that you have a very happy life."

Again the beggar gave a very surprising answer, "I have never had an unhappy day in my life."

At this, John Tauler looked at him and said, "How is that? What do you mean?"

The beggar replied, "When things are fine, I praise God. When there is rain, I praise God. When I have plenty, I praise God. When I have nothing, I praise God. God's will is my will. God's work in me is my work; therefore, I am never unhappy."

John Tauler could not believe his words and impulsively blurted out, "Who are you?"

The beggar straightened to full stature and regally exclaimed, "I am a king!"

Tauler laughed. "How can you be a king when you are dressed in ragged and tattered clothes and live as a beggar?"

Without hesitation, the beggar answered, "In my heart! In my heart!"[3]

This is how we keep our joy. His kingdom is in our hearts, and we live as His friends in privilege.

A WITNESS IN TESTIMONY

*For you will be His witness to all men of what you
have seen and heard* (Acts 22:15).

Fifth, a disciple is a *witness in testimony*. As used in this sense,
the Greek word is *martus* and means "to verify what one has
seen, heard, and experienced." A witness testifies to possessed
knowledge and faithfully interprets that knowledge in the light of
God's counsel and will.

In the context of Acts 22, Paul demonstrated this principle by
giving witness to his dramatic conversion. His witnessing ultimately caused such an uproar that a conspiracy, involving more
than forty men, was formed to kill him (see Acts 23:13). Paul had
to be escorted to Caesarea to relieve the tension and assure his
rights.

Even in the midst of this kind of life-and-death situation, however, this apostle exhibited calm assurance, an attitude that resulted from his willingness to be a witness. Paul's faithful witness
to what he received in Christ brought the confirmation of God's
favor. "The Lord stood by him and said, 'Be of good cheer, Paul;
for as you have testified for Me in Jerusalem, so you must also
bear witness at Rome'" (Acts 23:11).

This is one of the keys to keeping our joy—receiving the courage of the Lord and living our lives as faithful witnesses to His
work in us.

Steve Shelton witnessed to this in a stirring testimony of his
encounter with a waiter who noticed his depressed attitude. Inquiry brought out his embittered story of promiscuity, divorce,
and contemplated suicide.

To Steve's surprise, the waiter confidently said, "I know a person who can solve your problems, and His name is Jesus Christ."
Fascinated by such an answer, he asked for more information.

Later, when there was some time to talk privately, he was led to pray for salvation.

In his words,

> That was the major turning point of my life. I left that restaurant that day with a new purpose and direction for my life. Now, two years later, I am back on top in business; I am no longer seeking tawdry thrills; I am serving as an usher in church. Even my ex-wife and I are communicating on friendlier terms after a very stormy divorce.

This was a new beginning for Steve Shelton—and all because of a witnessing waiter.

It's true. The *witnessing* life is a *joyful* life.

A STEWARD IN TRUST

As each one has received a gift, minister it to one another, as good stewards of the manifold grace of God (1 Pet. 4:10).

Sixth, a disciple is a *steward in trust*. Here the Greek word is *ŏikŏnŏmŏs*. Denoting care, administration, and coordination of family affairs, the word technically refers to a person who manages a household. Theologically, however, the word refers to the appropriate use of God's gifts and the use of personal talents.

In this theological context, the apostle Peter wrote to people who had been dispersed throughout Asia Minor because of their witness for Christ and subsequent persecution. It is significant that Peter urged them to use their gifts as though they were managing them for God. In effect, he said that the good life is a productive life, and a productive life is a stewardship life.

A man named Harry illustrates this principle of stewardship. He wrote his life's story and entitled it "My Wheelchair to the

Stars." We don't usually think of climbing to the stars in a wheel-chair, but Harry did. At seven years of age he had rheumatic fever, and he later developed severe arthritis. His pain was so severe that often even the wearing of clothes was a torture.

He grew up in a textile town and had to be left alone while his mother and father worked to earn enough money to buy food and pay the medical bills. As Harry grew older, his illness bothered him until he began to feel very sorry for himself. He became bitter because he thought his life counted for little. He saw no reason to live. He never enjoyed a normal teenage life. He never dated, and he had few friends. He thought he was nothing but a burden to the world in general. He became fearful of what would become of him when he grew up, and he wondered how he would take care of himself.

One day he had a particularly bad experience. He fell out of his chair and lay helplessly on the floor for several hours. He said:

> I could not rise. I struggled and sweated and wept. There on the floor I battled again and again the black wave of bitterness. If I ever prayed, I prayed then. Eventually the postman came. I yelled to him and he came in and picked me up. As he helped me, he reminded me that "with God all things are possible" (Mark 10:27).[4]

These words literally changed Harry's outlook. He began to think about the possibility of what God could do for him.

Someone suggested that Harry learn how to paint Christmas cards. It took him six months to make his first cards, which he sold for only a nickel each, but he kept at it. In the first year he made $100 profit. The following year he took what seemed like a reckless plunge. He persuaded his father and mother to mortgage their home for $2,800. Harry borrowed another $1,000 and financed a mail-order greeting card business. His parents became concerned and asked, "If you don't sell the cards you have bought, what then?" Harry simply replied, "With God, all things are possible." He did sell the cards, and in the second year he did a million dollars' worth of business. No wonder Harry could write about going to the stars in a wheelchair. This man learned how to keep his joy by utilizing his best resources as a steward in trust.

A LIGHT IN INFLUENCE

You are the light of the world. A city that is set on a hill cannot be hidden. Nor do they light a lamp and put it under a basket, but on a lampstand, and it gives light to all who are in the house. Let your light so shine before men, that they may see your good works and glorify your Father in heaven (Matt. 5:14–16).

Finally, a disciple is a *light in influence*. The Greek word involved in verses 14 and 16 is *phŏs*. Light has always been used as a symbol of rank, influence, and power. God always reveals the very essence of His personality as light. Light fully discloses the message of God and its impact and power. Thus, when we walk in the light, we walk in sincerity. We take our Christian responsibility seriously. We recognize our insufficiency and place our full dependency upon the power of God through Christ in us.

In this regard, the most important part of us is our *influence*. As long as there is an automobile, Henry Ford lives. As long as there is an airplane, the Wright brothers live. As long as there is a light bulb, Thomas Edison lives. As long as there is electricity, Benjamin Franklin lives. Each of these men made a lasting impact on the world. In a secular sense, each one of them was a light to the world, a city set on a hill that could not be hidden.

Joy comes when we know we are bringing light to dark places and influencing our own private worlds for positive development.

Sometimes we take the power of influence too lightly. We forget that the only significant spiritual deed accomplished by Andrew was bringing his brother, Simon Peter, to Christ. But look what Peter accomplished!

In Reformation times, John Calvin was a tremendous light in influence. Among his significant spiritual deeds, he founded Geneva—the city of God. The truth, however, is that the influencing factor in John Calvin's life was a man named Farel.

One day while traveling from Paris to Strasbourg, Calvin stopped at the home of his friend, William Farel, in Geneva. While Calvin was there, Farel tried to persuade him to stay in Geneva and help to establish a model city. Calvin refused because he wanted to continue his private life in Strasbourg. Farel prayed all night that God would prevail upon John Calvin to remain in Geneva. The next morning Farel explained to Calvin that he felt that it was God's will for Calvin to stay and found a city based on spiritual principles. Calvin refused again, but later reconsidered. It was not long after that he established permanent residence in Geneva and gained control. On one occasion John Calvin said, "I felt as though the words of Farel were the very words of God Almighty speaking to me."

It appears that God gave Calvin a direct message through Farel to found the city of God in Geneva. Calvin became an influence in light because Farel was willing to share the light he had received from God. Joy is the knowledge that we are walking in the light even as He is in the light (see 1 John 1:7).

Any way we look at it, Christ has called us to a life of discipleship, which is a life full of meaning. Joy is maintained only as we make a conscious decision to live out that discipleship as believers in faith, servants in responsibility, branches in union, friends in privilege, witnesses in testimony, stewards in trust, and lights in influence.

3 *Stress Point*

Negative Thought Responses

TRANSFORMING YOUR THINKING

Scriptural
Source
Acts 27:20–36

Joy
Sustainers
Keep your head
Keep your heart
Keep your hope

3

TRANSFORMING YOUR THINKING

It was a long, fearful struggle with the tempest. The winds blew a gale; the waves ran wild and high; the rain poured down in torrents; the angry elements beat with ceaseless rage upon the torn sail, the shattered mast, and the reeling deck. The groaning timbers parted and let in water as fast as a hundred hands could bail it out. Everybody on board was wet—through and through. There was no opportunity to take food or rest. There they were—two hundred and seventy-six passengers and crew members with a load of wheat and a prisoner-preacher. They had been driven by the storm fourteen days and nights, helplessly, in a canalboatlike scow, which was bluntly rounded at both ends with no shaped and sharpened lines to cut the water. One lumbering mast stood upright in the middle, and it scarcely could stand the battering of the terrific fall winds.

It became so bad that all hope was lost—apparently the ship would crash on the rocky seashore. Then the prisoner-preacher—the apostle Paul, headed for Rome to face Emperor Nero on charges of blasphemy and heresy—took charge.

Everything was bedlam. The captain and crew were in a state of panic. With confident, authoritative words piercing through the howling winds, the apostle exclaimed, "And now I urge you to take heart, for there will be no loss of life among you, but only of the ship" (Acts 27:22).

Sounds encouraging! But, how did Paul know? How did he speak with such confidence? How did he keep his joy in such circumstances?

The apostle explained:

> For there stood by me this night an angel of the God to whom I belong and whom I serve, saying, "Do not be afraid, Paul; you must be brought before Caesar; and indeed God has granted you all those who sail with you" (Acts 27:23,24).

Sounds okay! However, it is a double message: *You will be saved, Paul, so you can die later at the hands of Nero.*

At first glance we may think that such a message doesn't make much sense. But then Paul exemplified that kind of inner attitude that transcends all of life's double messages and contradictions. He said, "Therefore take heart, men, for I believe God that it will be just as it was told me" (Acts 27:25).

Somehow this man of God named Paul had a thinking process that enabled him to keep his joy in the toughest of situations. His faith saw him through to the end that "they all escaped safely to land" (Acts 27:44).

A MATTER OF THE MIND

How can we, as twentieth-century people living in a tempestuous world, handle our personal storms with courage of heart and faith in God? Such an outlook is a matter of the mind—*a pattern of transformed thinking.*

No wonder the Bible tells us that as a person thinks, so he is (see Prov. 23:7), and it is apparent that is why the apostle Paul called for a *spiritual* mind (see Rom. 8:6), a *renewed* mind (see Eph. 4:23), a *transformed* mind (see Rom. 12:2), a *Christlike* mind (see 1 Cor. 2:16), and a *sound* mind (see 2 Tim. 1:7). Paul knew

For God has not given us a spirit of timidity, but of power and love and discipline.

that the only way to maintain joy is to live a life of transformed thinking.

A British grandmother applied this process of transformed thinking during World War II. At the very height of the London blitz, she refused to leave her downtown flat.

Practically every day, her son would urge her to move to his suburban home—located a much safer distance from the intensity of the bombing. Stubbornly, she refused. After all, she could not leave her work helping the wounded and the homeless. She was needed. Besides, she trusted the words of a plaque on her wall: DON'T WORRY! IT MAY NEVER HAPPEN! Constantly, she referred her son and family to the motto and reassured them that all would be well.

Then one day it happened—her apartment complex was hit. Two-thirds of the building was demolished. The son's family rushed to her flat as soon as they heard the news. They found her rocking in her favorite chair and singing her favorite hymn. Debris was strewn all about her.

In exasperation the son shouted at her, "Now what about your motto? It didn't see you through!"

"Oh, my goodness," she exclaimed, "I forgot to turn it over." She turned from her chair and flipped the plaque to the opposite side. There in shining letters it said, DON'T WORRY! YOU CAN TAKE IT!

This is the message of transformed thinking. It is a double message: "Don't worry! It may never happen! Don't worry! You can take it!

A MESSAGE OF MEANING

In reality, the power of transformed thinking is found in the degree of meaning it brings to our lives. Thus, when Paul told us not to be conformed to this world but to be transformed by the renewing of our minds (see Rom. 12:2), he was saying that we are to fulfill the will of God. This is where the essential meaning of life is found—in the "good and acceptable and perfect will of God."

Consequently, when we talk about the will of God, it is not simply with regard to careers, vocations, relationships, and everyday decisions. The will of God is for us to be like Christ (see Rom. 8:28–30), to strive to live by the mind of Christ. As Paul told the Corinthians, "We have the mind of Christ" (1 Cor. 2:16).

What this really tells us is that the mind of Christ is an attitude. We are what our attitudes make us, and by definition, attitudes involve our emotional, intellectual, and spiritual perceptions of life. Attitudes are formed by our tendencies to accept or reject certain individuals, groups, ideas, values, concepts, and social institutions. Attitudes literally involve the way we look at life in all of its complexity and variety.

Christ models this truth. The first recorded words we have from His boyhood are, "I must be about My Father's business" (Luke 2:49). Later, during His early ministry, He told His disciples, "My food is to do the will of Him who sent Me" (John 4:34), or, to paraphrase, "The very essence of My life is to do the will of the Father." At Capernaum, which became His hometown and the scene of most of His miracles, He proclaimed, "I do not seek my own will but the will of the Father who sent Me" (John 5:30). At Jerusalem He made it very clear that His work was to do God's will (see John 4:34). As He prepared to face His death, He said, "I have finished the work which You have given Me" (John 17:4). When Christ talked about His death, His resurrection, and His ultimate return, He didn't describe them as events He was planning or suggesting. Rather, He talked about them as a series of eternal imperatives necessary for Him to fulfill the will of the Father. This commitment to God's will gave Christ the power to face the Cross with joy (see Heb. 12:2).

Here is the message of meaning—*we keep our joy through attitudes that reflect the mind of Christ.*

This is what happened in the life of one woman. As she read my name on my lapel tag at a convention, she immediately threw her arms around me in a bear hug.

In surprise I drew back and said, "What does that mean?" With a rush of words and a glow on her face, she said:

> A couple of years ago I heard you speak at a rally. At that time I was suicidal. I was strung out on a combination of tran- quilizers, barbiturates, and alcohol. I was literally killing myself through drug abuse and was nothing but a vegetable with no purpose, no hope, and no future.
>
> Coerced by a friend, I reluctantly came to the rally and heard you talk about the fact that I could have a new mind through Christ. I thought to myself, *Is that really possible?* I began to pray to God that somehow He would renew my mind and give me power over all the suffering and hurt which were at the very base of my drug problems.
>
> When the time came for you to share with people in prayer, I was the first to raise my hand. Something dynamic took place in my mind. Since that day I have made a successful comeback to meaningful living. I literally received the mind of Christ. Now I am delivered from drugs and set free from my depression. I have this good job, and I've always said to myself, "If I ever see that Dr. Walker, I'm going to give him a big hug." That is what I just did.

The mind of Christ is the resource of joy. Paul found this out in the storm. Without the mind of Christ he never would have been sensitive to the revelation of the Lord through the angel. The voice of God would have meant nothing.

Here is Paul's formula for keeping joy through transformed thinking:

STEP ONE: KEEP YOUR HEAD

Now when neither sun nor stars appeared for many days, and no small
tempest beat on us, all hope that we would be saved was finally given
up. But after long abstinence from food, then Paul stood in the
midst of them and said, "Men, you should have listened
to me, and not have sailed from Crete and incurred this
disaster and loss. And now I urge you to take heart,
for there will be no loss of life among you, but only
of the ship" (Acts 27:20–22).

Paul could have despaired. He could have said, "Oh, God, what kind of God are You to bring me to this point?" He could have said, "God, if this is the best You have for me, I don't want to serve." He could have said, "God, what great sin have I committed that You would bring this calamity on me?" He could have said, "God, You know I have not sinned, and I have done nothing but good works for You. Why am I suffering in this storm?"

Paul could have lost his head, but he didn't. He didn't blow his cool. He didn't lose his bearings. He kept his reason. Paul knew that there is no gold without the fire of a refinery, no steel without the heat of a blast furnace, no diamond without the sharpness of a cutter's tool, no statue without the hammer and chisel of a sculptor, no faith without the fury of a storm.

How do we keep our heads? We internalize the Word! Psalm 48:9 says, "We have thought, O God, on Your lovingkindness, / In the midst of Your temple." Proverb 12:5 says, "The thoughts of the righteous are right, / But the counsels of the wicked are deceitful." Philippians 4:8 says, "Whatever things are true, whatever things are noble, whatever things are just, whatever things are pure, whatever things are lovely, whatever things are of good report, if there is any virtue and if there is anything praiseworthy—meditate on these things."

The Darnall family learned to keep their heads and dwell on the positive. Their handsome fifteen-year-old son went skating and, in the excitement of tag racing with his friends, fell and hit his head. The result was paralysis from the neck down. The doctors told his parents, "We've done everything we can do. He will be paralyzed the rest of his life. Put him in an institution. He will be a vegetable. He will probably die within five years."

The mother refused such a negative prognosis. Her response was, "We're going to take him home and put him in his room where we will surround him with the mind of Christ. We are going to saturate him with the power of God, the love of Christ, and the ministry of the Holy Spirit. We are going to give him the privilege of living out the rest of his life in the context of a Christian faith in a loving family."

And that is exactly what they did. At last accounting he had just stood up before a minister to be married to the young woman he loved dearly. He has been made perfectly whole with the exception of a slight impairment on one side. He still walks with a cane, but he is getting stronger every day.

The members of this family kept their heads and surrounded this boy with the mind of Christ.

STEP TWO: KEEP YOUR HEART

For there stood by me this night an angel of the God to whom
I belong and whom I serve, saying, "Do not be afraid,
Paul; you must be brought before Caesar; and indeed
God has granted you all those who sail
with you" (Acts 27:23,24).

Do not be afraid! Keep up your courage! Keep your heart!
When we look at our world, keeping heart is not always easy.
A giant cloud of gloom seems to hang over the entire planet, and

anxiety appears to be the order of the day. In 1985 alone, over fifty-five million prescriptions were written for a tranquilizer drug called Valium. And Valium is only one among many such synthetics used to try to help us keep our hearts.

Presently, one out of every three hospital beds is occupied by a person who is suffering from an illness caused by alcohol or some other drug.

Every day we experience the threats of international disaster, the pressures of an urbanized, commuter lifestyle, the problems of maintaining economic stability, and the uncertainties of changing world governments. Sometimes we wonder if there is reliability anywhere. This is a menacing age, and we can easily lose heart.

It is as though the last-day prophecies of hearts failing from fear (see Luke 21:26) and the elect's being deceived (see Matt. 24:24) are rapidly closing in on us.

All of this combines to put an overload on the mind and an overstress on the body. Thus, we talk about a physical-chemical imbalance and an emotionally induced burnout. Our thinking is frustrated, our consciousness is confused, our memory is impaired, and our learning is inhibited.

It seems impossible for us to live up to the uniqueness that God has given us in the likeness of His own image. We talk about being made "a little lower than the angels" and being "crowned [with] glory and honor" (Ps. 8:5) and possessing dominion over all nature with all things under our feet (see Ps. 8:6). However, many of us find that making that claim a reality poses a problem. We find it difficult to draw on our God-given resources. *We lose heart because we fail to generalize through the mind of Christ.*

Our uniqueness is such that we can learn a concept and store it in our memory for frequent recall. In this way we can generalize one experience into many different situations and circumstances. This can be good news or bad news. We can use what we have learned from past experiences to progress into confidence or regress into fear and anxiety. But we tend to generalize fear rather than faith, worry rather than assurance, depression rather than happiness, frustration rather than peace.

As a result, we overload with negative thinking and short-circuit ourselves into losing heart.

Thankfully, however, we have a choice. There is a different story to be told. There is a place in Christ where we can share the position of the apostle Paul and keep heart. We can keep our joy by living in the mind of Christ with power to cope with whatever comes our way.

In Paul's eyes, this is the Roman Road. To keep heart means:

- *A new emotional response*—"Let love be without hypocrisy" (Rom. 12:9a).
- *A new moral response*—"Abhor what is evil. Cling to what is good" (Rom. 12:9b).
- *A new relationship response*—"Be kindly affectionate to one another with brotherly love, in honor giving preference to one another" (Rom. 12:10).
- *A new spiritual response*—"Not lagging in diligence, fervent in spirit, serving the Lord" (Rom. 12:11).
- *A new motivational response*—"Rejoicing in hope, patient in tribulation, continuing steadfastly in prayer" (Rom. 12:12).
- *A new benevolence response*—"Distributing to the needs of the saints, given to hospitality" (Rom. 12:13).
- *A new intellectual response*—"Do not be overcome by evil, but overcome evil with good" (Rom. 12:21).

Perhaps it boils down to the witness of a dying ten-year-old girl. She had Werdnig-Hoffman disease, a progressive muscular atrophy, and all had been done that could be done. Her parents had to watch helplessly as she struggled against the pulmonary infection that would prove fatal.

Her father and mother were standing at the hospital bed, and it was more than her mother could take. Suddenly, she broke into body-racking sobs. Grief, frustration, tension, confusion, and fatigue all seemed to rush to the surface at once.

The girl was roused by the disturbance and sensed what her mother was experiencing. Out of a wisdom far beyond her years, she said, "Don't worry, Mommy. God will take care of me."

This is how we keep our joy. We trust in the God who will take care of us. We keep our hearts!

STEP THREE: KEEP YOUR HOPE

And as day was about to dawn, Paul implored them all to take food, saying, "Today is the fourteenth day you have waited and continued without food, and eaten nothing. Therefore I urge you to take nourishment, for this is for your survival, since not a hair will fall from the head of any of you." And when he had said these things, he took bread and gave thanks to God in the presence of them all; and when he had broken it he began to eat. Then they were all encouraged, and also took food themselves
(Acts 27:33–36).

The formula is clear: A cool head plus a clean heart equals a confident hope. Paul expressed that hope to his fellow passengers, and they were all encouraged.

By definition, *hope* is "the confident expectation of fulfillment." It is desire plus emotion.

Too often we give up. We get caught in temporal timetables of our own making, like a get-rich-quick, instant-prosperity scheme. Then when it all doesn't come our way, we are prone not only to throw the cargo overboard but to jump in after it and sink to the bottom of the sea.

Sometimes we try hard to bring God down to us instead of our going up to God through Christ. We find ourselves reducing God to fit our own selfish traps—and we miss His best for us.

We need the power of confessing faith. We need the confidence of claiming God's promises. But above all else, we need the personal commitment to Christ whereby hope becomes our motivator; faith, our activator; and assurance, our ultimator. Commitment thereby enables not our ambition, but Christ's ambition in us; not our desire, but Christ's desire in us; not our goal, but Christ's goal in us; not our healing, but Christ's healing in us; not our miracle, but Christ's miracle in us.

This is the meaning of 2 Corinthians 2:14, "Now thanks be to God who always leads us in triumph in Christ, and through us diffuses the fragrance of His knowledge in every place." To triumph is to rise above. To triumph is to overcome. To triumph is to defeat. To triumph is to vanquish. To triumph is to keep joy through hope. This is the power of hope—to triumph in Christ.

In hope we *believe* (see Rom. 4:18); in hope we *receive* (see Rom. 8:24); in hope we *endure* (see Rom. 15:4); in hope we *survive* (see 1 Cor. 13:13); in hope we *testify* (see 1 Pet. 3:15); in hope we are *purified* (see 1 John 3:3).

In this context I have always been impressed with Helen Keller. Blind and deaf, she rose above her circumstances to make a mark on the world that will never be forgotten.

She became an eloquent speaker, yet never heard her own voice; she wrote nine books, yet never saw their bindings. She received an honorary doctorate from Glasgow University in Scotland and responded to an audience she could not see and a thundering applause she could not hear by saying, "Neither darkness nor silence can impede the progress of the human spirit."

She read her braille Bible so often that certain passages had been worn completely smooth. And when asked what she thought of Christ, she replied in confidence and assurance, "Jesus Christ in my life is triumphant love."

This is how we keep our joy: We transform our thinking by keeping our heads, our hearts, and our hope. Negative thoughts become a thing of the past as we adopt this way of thinking. Keeping our joy is a matter of the mind and a message of meaning.

4 *Stress Point*

Inefficient Speech Patterns

VITALIZING YOUR VOCABULARY

Scriptural Source

Ephesians 4:29,31,32

Joy Sustainers

Refine your thinking with words
Respect others with words
Relate to others with words
Reinforce positive feelings with words
Reflect compassion with words

4

VITALIZING YOUR VOCABULARY

God has given us a powerful mechanism called the human anatomy. The trick is learning how to channel the energies of this complex machine into a productive and joyous lifestyle.

In Genesis 1:27 we are assured that we are created "in the image of God." Again in Psalm 139:14, the Bible tells us that we are "fearfully and wonderfully made."

FEARFULLY AND WONDERFULLY MADE

To be fearfully and wonderfully made means that we have the capacity to reflect the very personhood of God. In a very real sense we have been created by the spark of the divine.

Physically, we have a skeletal system of 206 bones that enables us to walk, run, jump, and bend. We have a muscular system of over 600 muscles that gives us the capacity to manipulate those bones into different movements at the same time. We have a circulation network of 60,000 miles of tubing that transports the life flow of blood to all parts of the body. We have a nervous system made up of the brain, the spinal cord, and a vast network of nerves capable of sending impulses over 350 feet per second. We have a processing plant whereby we manufacture energy through respiration, digestion, and evacuation.

Intellectually, we reflect the image of God through our ability to reason, think, and calculate. We can solve problems, make decisions, and develop values to govern our lives.

Emotionally, we express the image of God in our capacity to experience, enjoy, and appreciate. We can experience the feelings of love, joy, and excitement as well as the feelings of anger, hate, and resentment. We can enjoy the beauty of a rose, the majesty of a mountain, and the glory of a sunset. We can appreciate the aesthetic qualities of an art masterpiece, the exquisite cut of a diamond, and the intricate harmonies of music.

Spiritually, we innately have a deep-seated desire to be in relationship with God. Every civilization on earth has made an attempt to be in communication with a higher power. Something deep within us longs for redemption and reconciliation with the Creator.

AS THE TONGUE GOES

No doubt about it. We are fearfully and wonderfully made in the image of God. The tongue is the smallest yet, in many ways, the most powerful part of God's image in us. And as the tongue goes, so goes the body, the intellect, the emotions, and the spirit. The way we speak is the way we live, think, act, and relate.

It is true that *we are what we speak*. This is why Proverb 17:27 tells us that the person of knowledge "spares his words" and the person of understanding "is of a calm spirit." This is what Colossians 4:6 means when we are admonished to let our "speech always be with grace, seasoned with salt" so that we can give an appropriate answer to everyone.

James gave strong warnings about the tongue. To him, the

"tongue is a fire, a world of iniquity. . . . It defiles the whole body, and sets on fire the course of nature; and it is set on fire by hell. . . . It is an unruly evil, full of deadly poison" (James 3:6,8). Further, James viewed the tongue as the agency of hypocrisy, and he made the statement that "with it we bless our God and Father, and with it we curse men, who have been made in the similitude of God." The tragedy is that "out of the same mouth proceed blessing and cursing" (James 3:9,10).

We can lose our joy by the way we speak. James told us we need a vitalized vocabulary that gives us the power to speak the words of joy and productive living. In his description, negative speech patterns produce bitter envy and selfish ambitions, which result in disorder and evil practice. On the other hand, James encouraged us to develop positive speech patterns that bring the wisdom that comes from heaven. This wisdom is pure, peaceable, gentle, willing to yield, full of mercy and good fruits, impartial, and sincere. The result is that we can become peacemakers who sow in peace and raise a harvest of righteousness (see James 3:17,18).

THE VITALIZED VOCABULARY

If we want joy in our hearts, joy in our homes, joy in our businesses, joy in our automobiles, joy in our relationships, we have to speak those things that produce joy. We have to speak words that are pure, peaceable, gentle, willing to yield, full of mercy and good fruits, impartial, and sincere. We literally vitalize our vocabularies by embracing a speech pattern that communicates all the positive virtues that enhance and strengthen.

But this brings up a problem with translation. How do we get it from theory into practice?

Putting a vitalized vocabulary into action is our basic problem. Too often we are like the little boy in Sunday school. When asked the memory verse of the day, he answered by saying, "I don't remember the verse, but I do remember the zip code—John 3:16." Sometimes we remember the zip codes, but we forget the message.

However, the apostle Paul had the message, and in his epistle to the Ephesians he gave us a formula for the translation:

> Let no corrupt word proceed out of your mouth, but what is good for necessary edification, that it may impart grace to the hearers (Eph. 4:29).

What does this formula mean in terms of joy? Let's break it down into smaller components and examine each one.

A VITALIZED VOCABULARY REFINES

Let no corrupt word proceed out of your mouth . . .

The key word here is *corrupt*. In the New Testament, the Greek word is *saprös,* which technically means "anything that is rotten, bad, worthless, or corrupt." The starting point, then, is one of self-control. We need to take charge of our mouths! And we can start by not allowing anything rotten to be reflected in our speech.

We claim to be a Christian nation. We even inscribe IN GOD WE TRUST on our coins. Yet, we have to rate our movies and monitor our television shows because of unrefined language.

When our language is unrefined, we become *aggressive* and verbally attack one another. We become loud, harsh, and demanding. We revert to hostile expressions and find ourselves being isolated from others because of our debilitating talk.

When our language is unrefined, we become *irresponsible*. We erroneously repeat things we hear. We join the gossip circuit and assassinate character through devastating innuendos without the true facts. Unrefined language overstates, misrepresents, and discolors.

It is so easy to ruin others with words. In some cases, we divorce because of words; we lose lifelong friends because of words; we lose businesses because of words; we even start wars because of words.

It is amazing how stories get started. As a case in point, I once spent about eight days in the hospital—five days one week and three days two weeks later.

Because of fatigue, I suffered a vertigo attack, and the doctor put me in the hospital to check out a heart click he heard in the examination. Since I had never had a thorough heart check, I was put through all the paces including a catheterization. All the tests turned out clear—no heart blockage or impairment. The click remains and has been diagnosed as a "floppy valve," a nonproblematic condition experienced by thousands.

It later became apparent that a hematoma (a swelling containing blood) had developed on the artery because of the trauma of the catheterization. I was hospitalized for monitoring. This condition, too, proved negligible, and I was released after three days. Since that time, all has normalized, and I have had no complications.

The stories started almost the moment I was first hospitalized. One telephone caller stated that I had suffered a massive heart attack and would never preach again. Another report, to my eighty-three-year-old mother, described in detail my terrible nervous breakdown that would require a year's leave of absence. A third story that made the ministerial circuit gave an account of my drug addiction; I was supposed to be hospitalized for a drying-out period that would be followed by my rehabilitation in an institution. One man called to find out the name of my successor. Sounds like the old parlor game in which the guests divide into two groups and each group is given a secret to be passed from person to person. After the secret has been relayed to each person, the last person of the group openly states the secret. In almost every case, the last account has little resemblance to the original secret.

A vitalized vocabulary, however, refines, and joy is maintained when no corrupt word proceeds out of our mouths.

A VITALIZED VOCABULARY RESPECTS

. . . but what is good . . .

Respecting others is the second step. The important word here is *edification*. By definition, *to edify*, as used in this context, means "to build." Edification lifts up, shores up, raises, and brings into symmetry and balance. Thus, to respect is to build others up and to accept others as being important in the image of God—even when we don't agree with certain behaviors, attitudes, and values.

Somewhere in our society we have lost the importance of respect, and this loss shows in the maintenance of our cities. It is apparent in the attitudes of businesses toward customers and of customers toward businesses. It is nonexistent in many homes between parents and children. We seem to have a penchant for defacement, abuse, ridicule, and the profaning of those things that are holy and sacred. The tough part is that this disrespect is reflected in our speech. Irreverence for God and His holy Trinity is taken for granted as acceptable and normal. In fact, a mark of sophistication in many circles is the ability to speak profanity in a unique or unusual way.

The experience of a consultant who flew to Atlanta to share

with our church in a Christian education conference illustrates this prevalent mind-set.

When my associate and I met her at the airport, her first words were, "My goodness! Did I just have an interesting experience!"

Upon our inquiry, she related a series of events that started when a hostile and irritated business executive was seated by her on the plane. Because of mechanical problems, his private Lear jet had been grounded at the last minute, and he was forced not only to ride on a commercial plane, but to travel tourist class because the first-class section was sold out.

As a result, he was loud and boisterous, and he used the Lord's name in vain every other breath. Finally, the consultant could contain herself no longer and politely asked him, "Sir, do you always pray like that? During the past few minutes, you have asked God to do some very horrible things to this plane and a lot of different people. If He were to answer those prayers, all of our lives would be in jeopardy."

Obviously, this was a new twist for a man who was late to an important executive meeting—a crucial meeting with his salesmen. Stymied by her seeming impertinence, he asked what she meant by such a statement.

Given this opening, she shared a whole new way of life that could be found through peace in Christ. He was fascinated. He even repeated after her certain passages of Scripture from the New Testament that spoke directly to his need.

As often happens, the Holy Spirit convicted his heart. He made a profession of faith and invited the consultant to speak to all his salesmen at his next quarterly meeting.

As 2 Corinthians 5:17 states, "Old things have passed away; behold, all things have become new." In the executive's case, it was a deliverance from the profane and a development of the reverent. The end result was a new kind of speech that motivates joy as it builds up others in faith and peace.

We have to speak with respect if we are to keep our joy. Irreverent speech breeds guilt, fear, suspicion, and distrust. Respect says I'm going to build you up . . . I cherish you . . . I want to clarify your feelings and needs . . . I want to relate to you in an interpersonal and empathetic way . . . I want to motivate your cooperation . . . I want you to join me in working out this problem . . . I care for you . . . I sense your hurt . . . I want to build you up.

A VITALIZED VOCABULARY RELATES

. . . for necessary edification . . .

Speech patterns often mean the difference between meaningful or conflicting relationships. The way we talk is the way we relate, and the way we relate is a joy activator or detractor.

It is tragic, but true, that the number one personality problem of the eighties has been identified as *narcissism,* a Greek mythological term for selfishness. When we live narcissistically, we have grandiose ideas of our own importance. We nurture those ideas by an overexaggeration of our own abilities, talents, and accomplishments as well as by a preoccupation with such things as our brilliance, success, power, and status. The result is a lack of empathy for others and a drive for success, regardless of who gets hurt.

Ultimately, this means disillusionment and loss of joy, but the apostle Paul talked about a better way and described a love that relates to the needs of others. This love "suffers long . . . is kind . . . does not envy . . . does not parade itself . . . is not puffed up

. . . does not behave rudely . . . does not seek its own . . . is not provoked . . . thinks no evil . . . does not rejoice in iniquity, but rejoices in the truth . . . bears all things . . . believes . . . hopes . . . endures . . . never fails" (1 Cor. 13:4–8).

This passage became the textbook for a hard-nosed but diamond-in-the-rough construction worker who walked unannounced into an office. With tears in his eyes he blurted out to the minister, "Teach me the language of love."

Startled by such a statement from such a man, the minister replied, "I'm not sure what you mean. Apparently you're really hurting and having trouble expressing your true feelings."

With this he broke into sobs and told a tragic story of a rough man with a profane mouth who was married to a sensitive woman with a desire to live the Christian life.

For many years he had been a verbal abuser, and his speech was constantly highlighted by the dirtiest and foulest descriptions. Finally, his wife had enough, and they were divorced.

After a year of living alone and trying the swinging single life, he wanted his wife back, but she refused to consider reconciliation until he demonstrated a *new kind of walk* with a *new kind of talk*.

In his search to be different, he attended church. On a particular day of conflict, after his former wife had rebuffed him stiffly, he came to the end of his road and sought out the minister for help. He wanted to learn to speak the language of love.

It was hard for this tough man to learn to talk tenderly, but he gave it his best effort. Through a newfound faith in Christ, the support of a loving prayer group, and a rather long and painful period of counseling, the marriage was restored. He has had some stormy moments, but he is continuing to learn to speak the language of love, and she is learning to relate in a way that makes it worth his while to speak that language.

This couple is learning to talk "for necessary edification."

A VITALIZED VOCABULARY REINFORCES

. . . that it may impart grace to the hearers.

In this passage the key word is *grace,* derived from the Greek word *charis,* which refers to graciousness of manner or act or to gratitude (acceptable, benefit, favor, gift). It has been said that the most powerful human force in the world is the ability to positively reinforce.

Contrary to many opinions, behavior is not changed by punishment. Punishment may start or stop certain behaviors, but only reinforcement brings about true behaviorial change.

This is what Paul meant when he used the phrases "impart grace to the hearers." Grace means receiving a gift with no strings attached. Grace is God doing for us what we cannot do for ourselves. It is God's kindness to us in spite of our selfishness and sinfulness.

Perhaps this is the essential meaning of the cliché, Little things mean a lot. Words make or break us. The situation can be just right; the environment can be perfect; the setting can be flawless—yet, if we say the wrong words and fail to reinforce others with language that benefits, we can miss the magic moment and lose our joy.

This was the case of Carol who in anger and anxiety opened up her heart by saying,

Everything was perfect. It was a gorgeous night. We were sailing off the coast of Mexico. It was supposed to be a second honeymoon in which we could regain the closeness we had before the children came and the business grew. But right there in the most romantic time when everything was right to say those things I desperately needed to say and more desperately needed to hear, all we did was to rehash an old argument that brought back all the old feelings of resentment and bitterness. I blew my cool! He exploded! We both said a lot of hurtful things! I caught

64

an early plane home. We have separated, and I don't know if we can ever make it together again.

What a tragedy. All because of ill-chosen words and a lack of reinforcing attitudes that "impart grace."

But what a contrast is expressed in the following letter:

> I thought you might wonder sometimes what has happened to couples you've married. So I'm reporting back to you to let you know that my wife and I are doing great. Coming real soon it will be eleven months since you married us. We've learned a lot about each other to say the least. But each day we are growing in love more and more.
>
> We have experienced an exciting growth for both of us together in the Lord. I know that people would say, "They've only been married eleven months; give them time and the excitement will cease." However, it is our pledge to each other to always work together to keep our love strong.

Over half of all marriages end in divorce, and if the polls are correct, many people who continue to live together in marriage are unhappy and sometimes unfaithful.

Regrettably, we lose the vitalization of a reinforcing vocabulary that benefits those who listen. The solution is to capture the spirit of this young couple who have pledged themselves to always work to keep love strong. This is the power of reinforcement.

A VITALIZED VOCABULARY REFLECTS

*Let all bitterness, wrath, anger, clamor, and evil speaking be put
away from you, with all malice. And be kind to one another,
tenderhearted, forgiving one another, even as God
in Christ forgave you* (Eph. 4:31,32).

This succinct passage summarizes the formula for joyful living. We have to handle the negatives through the positive forces
of the power of Christ in us.

If we express ourselves in bitterness, wrath, anger, clamor,
and evil speaking, with all malice, we rob ourselves of the full
meaning of the joyful life.

Bitterness is a result of harboring hurts, disappointments, rejec-
tions, and conflicts. We repress the pain deep in the unconscious
mind, and bitterness has a way of finding expression in our attitudes, relationships, and general personality.

Wrath involves an uncontrolled temper that causes us to act
impetuously. Wrath is characterized as wind in violent motion,
such as a hurricane or tornado. In the *psychological* sense, wrath is
an inner conflict resulting in loss of control. In the *spiritual* sense,
wrath results in a strained relationship with Christ, which often
manifests itself in the behavior described by the apostle Paul in
Romans 7:15: "For what I am doing, I do not understand. For
what I will to do, that I do not practice; but what I hate, that I
do."

Anger involves a hostile reaction to a painful outside circumstance, experience, or person. When uncontrolled, anger incites
us to seek revenge regardless of the cost. Aristotle described anger as a twofold response of desire and grief. His interpretation
of the word is illustrated in Mark 3:5 when Christ was angered
by the hardness of heart exhibited by the scribes and Pharisees.
They complained because He healed on the Sabbath; Christ's

reaction was one of anger because He grieved for their lack of spiritual insight.

Clamor denotes a sense of unrestraint with little or no regard for others, while *evil speaking* concerns false witness and abuse against another person resulting in the wounding of reputation or the assassinating of character.

Malice indicates a mind-set bent on malevolence, immorality, and depraved desire. A malicious lifestyle is characterized by arrogance and violence.

The Bible, however, calls upon us to reflect the very image of Christ by expressing kindness and compassion to one another in an attitude of forgiveness that models after the work of Christ.

To be kind and *tenderhearted* is to furnish what is needed by others to enhance their joy and well-being. *To forgive* is to wipe the slate clean of any real or imaginary wrong so that the other person is as justified as if he or she had never committed the wrong in the first place.

This is what Christ has done for us. Our sins are as far removed as the East is from the West (see Ps. 103:12) and are put in the sea of God's forgetfulness (see Isa. 43:25). We have joy because we reflect the image of Christ.

On the one hand, if we speak bitterly, we breed alienation. If we speak wrathfully, we breed violence. If we speak angrily, we breed hostility. If we speak clamorously, we breed mistrust. If we speak evilly, we breed retaliation. If we speak maliciously, we breed disdain.

On the other hand, if we speak kindly and forgivingly, we breed the fruit of the Spirit in love, joy, peace, longsuffering, kindness, goodness, faithfulness, gentleness, and self-control (see Gal. 5:22,23). The crucified life controls the tongue and vitalizes the vocabulary.

How do we keep our joy? We vitalize our vocabularies with words that minister grace.

5 *Stress Point*

Low Self-Esteem

INTERNALIZING YOUR IMAGE

Scriptural
Sources

Ephesians 4:21–24
Romans 1:1–7

Joy
Sustainers

Emphasize the spiritual over the secular
Internalize the new over the old
Strive for the highest

5

INTERNALIZING YOUR IMAGE

If I asked you about what you want most in life, what would you answer? There would probably be as many answers as people; yet, one prevailing theme would be voiced by us all—namely, "I want to be happy!"

But what does happiness mean? Status? Career? Success? Family? Religion? Knowledge? Health? Service? Balance? All of the above? None of the above?

Somehow the quest for happiness has been almost as elusive as looking for a black cat in a dark basement when the cat isn't there. Alexander Pope, the famous English poet, expressed this thought by saying:

> O happiness! our being's end and aim!
> Good, pleasure, ease, content! whate'r thy name:
> That something still which prompts the eternal sigh,
> For which we bear to live, or dare to die.

The meaning of happiness may be nebulous for many people, but its pursuit seems to be all-consuming for most human beings.

In Christian circles we talk about joy and how to keep it. In secular circles we talk about pleasure and how to escalate it. But we all agree that there has to be more to happiness than just eating, drinking, breathing, thinking, working, and interacting.

Somewhere, somehow, there has to be meaning to what we are doing and why we are doing it. In the main, happiness is a sense of self-worth that enables us to feel that we have value to God, others, and ourselves.

In terms of Christian joy, happiness is the ability to handle pressure, cope with circumstances, and find solutions for negative situations. We lose our joy when we feel as if we are bearing the weight of the world and have lost our sense of control.

In this regard a woman flew into Atlanta from the East Coast. She sat in my office depressed, dejected, and disconsolate. She was so uptight she could scarcely stay seated for thirty seconds at a time. Consequently, she paced back and forth incessantly.

With anxiety in her voice and fear on her face, she haltingly said:

> I've enough money to live for the rest of my life without working another day. I have everything I want. I have been everywhere, seen everything, and experienced all there is to experience. Now, tell me, Dr. Walker, why am I so depressed and unhappy?

My first impulse was to respond, "I don't know, but I would like to try your lifestyle for a while to see." But hers was a serious and important question. The pollsters say that Americans who claim to be happy never quite get their fill. Too many folks always seem to experience an emotional letdown that in turn leads to a depressed state of mind.

Could it be that most of us look for happiness and joy in the wrong place? Are we trusting in the wrong source? Are we overlooking the most important aspect of keeping the joyful life—namely, the internalization of identity in the image of God? Can we really live a joyful life apart from God in Christ?

Glen had everything but what he needed the most—a sense of self-worth. When he was a child, his parents never praised him.

He always felt second-best to an older sister and crowded out by a younger brother. All his life he tried to win approval that never came.

He was a loner in his college years, and his peers overlooked him most of the time. He had few friends, seldom dated, and became a wallflower who lingered in the background while others received all the strokes for success and accomplishment. His closest friends were bought friends, and the majority of his relationships were fringe relationships.

He was passive in his marriage. As a consequence, his wife lost respect for him—and the result was a "cold-war" existence despite having brought three children into the world. His wife lived for the children; he lived for his business. Both were successful, but neither shared closeness.

When the children were grown, his wife divorced him and business boomed. But he felt like a nothing.

EMPHASIZE THE SPIRITUAL
OVER THE SECULAR

How do we get from a nothing to a something? Moving from nothing to something starts with perception. Do we see ourselves as spiritual or secular?

Glen lived by the secular and blocked out all the spiritual resources available to him.

The secular person accepts a way of life that denies the divine and refuses to accept the *spirit* of man as having validity.

To the secularist, man is the measure of all things.

To the secularist, God is the human power within personhood for potential development.

To the secularist, faith is a process of human experience.

To the secularist, morality is self defined, applied for one's own interest, and adapted to each situation for one's own favor. It is devoid of an absolute base.

The Bible makes it clear, however, that the most important aspect of human existence is the spirit of personhood.

This is the meaning of Job 32:8, "But there is a spirit in man, / And the breath of the Almighty gives him understanding."

This is the meaning of Ecclesiastes 12:7, "Then the dust [of the body] will return to the earth as it was, / And the spirit will return to God who gave it."

This is the meaning of James 2:26, "For as the body without the spirit is dead, so faith without works is dead also."

This is the meaning of Galatians 2:20, "I have been crucified with Christ; it is no longer I who live, but Christ lives in me; and the life which I now live in the flesh I live by faith in the Son of God, who loved me and gave Himself for me."

This is the meaning of John 15:11, "These things I have spoken to you, that My joy may remain in you, and that your joy may be full."

This is the meaning of Romans 8:6, "For to be carnally minded is death, but to be spiritually minded is life and peace."

True joy is a direct result of nurturing our spirits in the Christ image within us. We are made in the likeness of God (see Gen. 5:1); we are created a little lower than the angels and crowned with glory and honor (see Ps. 8:5); we are to be rulers over God's creation (see Ps. 8:6); we are the temple of the Spirit of God (see 1 Cor. 6:19); we are the very reflection of the glory of God (see 2 Cor. 3:18).

Without contradiction, history has demonstrated that when the spirit of man is ignored, education dies, crime increases, disease multiplies, wars escalate, and civilizations crumble.

This is why we are to honor God with our bodies and live to please the Spirit in such a way that we reap eternal life (see 1 Cor.

6:20; Gal. 6:8). We are to live on every word that comes from the mouth of God and to love God with all of our hearts, souls, minds, and strength so that we can be free persons showing proper respect to everyone (see Deut. 8:3; Mark 12:30,31; 1 Pet. 2:16).

The apostle Peter told us to be holy as God is holy and summarized our lifestyle by saying we are to live such good lives among the pagans that although we may be accused of doing wrong, they will ultimately see our good deeds and glorify God on the day He visits us (see 1 Pet. 1:16; 2:12).

INTERNALIZE THE NEW OVER THE OLD

Internalizing the new over the old sounds great. But how do we come to such high and lofty principles?

Glen had to learn that the only way he could move from his depressed, anxious state was to come into the new image of Christ that would give him power to eliminate his old way of thinking about life.

This is what the Bible is talking about in Ephesians 4:21-24,

[You] have been taught by Him, as the truth is in Jesus: that you put off, concerning your former conduct, the old man which grows corrupt according to the deceitful lusts, and be renewed in the spirit of your mind, and that you put on the new man which was created according to God, in true righteousness and holiness.

The process of keeping our joy involves putting off the old self and putting on the new self, which strives for Christ likeness in the development of new attitudes, beliefs, and values.

In Glen's case, he struggled for about a year, but grew; finally, the time came when he was able to translate the resources of

God's Word into his everyday life. In his words, "At long last I feel that I have arrived at the place that I can look myself in the mirror and feel good about myself in every way."

We can transcend the forces that have impeded our growth. We are more than what our limitations have forced us to be. We are more than what our thought patterns have restricted us to.

We are *character*—made in the image of God in righteousness and holiness.

We are *adjustment*—capable of reconciling with God, ourselves, and the world in peace regardless of the past.

We are *interests*—designed to pursue personalized goals and dreams through the resources given to us by our relationship to God through Christ in His Word.

We are *attitudes*—motivated to respond to life in mental and emotional patterns that reflect the very Spirit of Christ.

We are *temperament*—balanced by the emotional tone of the Holy Spirit, who enables us to maintain equilibrium in the midst of life's fluctuations.

The danger is that we claim the new self in Christ but continue to live by the patterns of the old self. When we live by the old life, we become part of the statistics that speak of worry, tension, fear, and anxiety. Some of the most recent facts released by the Mental Health Association of Atlanta give some startling and sobering insights:

- In any 6-month period, approximately 29.4 million adult Americans (18.7 percent of the population) suffer from one or more mental disorders.
- For men, the most frequent disorders are alcohol abuse/ dependence, phobia, drug abuse/dependence and dysthymia (despondency).
- For women, the most frequent disorders are phobia, major depressive episodes without grief, dysthymia and obsessive-compulsive disorders.

- People aged 25 to 44 accounted for the largest percentage of admissions to all inpatient psychiatric services in 1980 (latest figures).
- Suicides by persons under the age of 35 increased markedly between 1958 and 1982 from 19 to 41 percent. Suicide was the third leading cause of death for the age group in 1982.
- Fewer than one-fifth of the individuals identified with any mental disorder in a 6-month period used any mental health service from either mental health specialists or general medical physicians.
- For each type of inpatient psychiatric service, more than 70 percent of admissions were readmissions to inpatient psychiatric care.
- Schizophrenia was the most frequent primary diagnosis for admissions to state and county mental hospitals and public and multiservice non-Federal general hospitals; affective disorders, for admissions to private psychiatric hospitals and nonpublic, non-Federal general hospitals; and alcohol-related disorders, for admissions to VA medical centers.
- There were 53 percent fewer psychiatric beds available in 1982 than in 1970.
- During 1980 (latest figures), total expenditures for mental health care in the United States were estimated to be between $19.4 and $24.1 billion.
- The expenditures represent approximately 7.7 percent of total expenditures for general health care and approximately 0.7 percent of the nation's Gross National Product.
- Of these expenditures, approximately 53.6 percent were incurred in the specialty mental health sector, 30.6 percent in the general health sector and 15.8 in the human services and nonhealth sector.
- On the average, state mental health agencies spent 66.5 percent of their budgets in state mental hospitals and 29.7 per-

cent in community-based programs, but there was great variability across states.

• Per capita expenditures across states range from a high of $66.74 to a low of $7.90, with a national average of $24.30.[1]

All of the above is a classic depiction of "no joy."

As one pastor put it during a heartrending counseling session, "I preach it, sing it, and teach it to others, but somehow I keep letting the old life dominate my thoughts and attitudes."

At one point this pastor's ambivalence and depression became so acute that he suffered severe abdominal pain.

The doctors made all the tests, prescribed a variety of drugs, and suggested many types of therapy, but no long-term help resulted. Finally, the doctors decided to do exploratory surgery to find out what could possibly be the cause of such an acute condition.

During the interim period before surgery, we happened to talk together. In the course of the conversation I suggested that his physical problems might be caused by carrying the weight of everyone's problems while continuing to live by his old-self resources. Perhaps he needed to allow the new image of Christ to be internalized in every area of his life.

Knowing his temperament and personality, I could not help sharing that I was reminded of the illustration of Atlas holding up the world. Every time we talked he was burdened with other people's problems and the imponderable difficulties of the world at large. At one point I had a sudden inspiration, and I talked him into writing down on a piece of paper, "I hereby resign from assuming the responsibility of God."

Then we went to the Word and reaffirmed the importance of knowing our true positions in Christ. Romans 1:1–7 spoke directly to his need from the experience of the apostle Paul:

> Paul, a bondservant of Jesus Christ, called to be an apostle, separated to the gospel of God which He promised before through

His prophets in the Holy Scriptures, concerning His Son Jesus Christ our Lord, who was born of the seed of David according to the flesh, and declared to be the Son of God with power according to the Spirit of holiness, by the resurrection from the dead. Through Him we have received grace and apostleship for obedience to the faith among all nations for His name, among whom you also are the called of Jesus Christ;

To all who are in Rome, beloved of God, called to be saints.

Paul had every reason to have an absolutely miserable attitude and negative lifestyle. Yet, he found a powerful paradox of life that enabled him to say in 2 Corinthians 6:10, "as sorrowful, yet always rejoicing; as poor, yet making many rich; as having nothing, and yet possessing all things."

The secret to this type of joyful living is that Paul saw himself as a servant who had found new life by submitting his will totally to God's will. He saw himself as an apostle or an ambassador of Christ with an urgent message for all the world to hear. He saw himself as a part of the body of Christ whereby he belonged to Christ, was loved by God, and called to live a consecrated life.

Finally, Colossians 3:3,4 became the motivating point for this pastor truly to break from the old self and put on the new self. In this passage the apostle Paul gave the secret to successful joyful living when he emphatically stated to the Colossians specifically and to us generally, "For you died, and your life is hidden with Christ in God. When Christ, who is our life appears, then you also will appear with Him in glory."

Through the work of the Holy Spirit in a willing and searching heart, the message took root, and this pastor's heart was truly hidden with Christ. He decided to set a new course of personal living, postponed the exploratory operation, and within two months found himself pain-free with a new lease on life.

In his words, "I decided to internalize Christ into all the areas of my life. As a result, I began to practice what I preached and became a brand-new person."

STRIVE FOR THE HIGHEST

In spite of all of his adversity, Paul had a handle on joy and made it work in his life because he internalized the image of Christ. He knew that he had been made new in the attitudes of his mind and had put on the new self.

There was another dimension, however, in his example. Paul said that we are "created according to God, in true righteousness and holiness" (Eph. 4:24).

To be like *(according to)* God is a big order. What do we have to do to be like God. The key words are *righteousness* and *holiness*.

To be righteous is to line up our lives with the claims and principles of a higher authority. It is to have a sense of moral integrity that reflects the very nature of God. It is to accept eagerly and joyfully the responsibilities God gives us through His Word as the essence of productive living.

In the practical sense, righteousness completes assignments, keeps promises, pays bills, honors commitments, keeps appointments, strives to be on time, and establishes a reputation of reliability.

To be holy is to live out this righteousness in an observable way so that people will see our good works and glorify God (see 1 Pet. 2:12). To be holy is to be set apart or consecrated for service in the kingdom. It is a behavioral style that thinks like God, loves what God loves, hates what God hates, relates to other people as God has related to us, and acts like God acts.

This was the case of Beth, a trying-to-reform hooker. She came for counseling with resistance but a sense of, If this doesn't work, I'm going to end it all.

She said, "I see all of you pious Christians coming together every Sunday to go through your rituals, but I wonder, Is there really anything to knowing God, or is it all one big game that people play?"

On the one hand, she was tired of her sordid life and had come to the point where the oldest profession in the world was not paying off as it once had. She was becoming one of the oldest people in her profession.

On the other hand, she was frightened, bitter, and angry about life in general and toward God in particular.

How could she be like God? After all, she was living the life of the lowest of the low, and she knew it.

After a few sessions, it boiled down to a question of image. Would she accept the fact that she could truly become a new person in Christ? Would she allow the forgiveness of Christ to erase all her old life and replace it with a new life like God?

The biblical witnesses of Mary Magdalene (see Luke 8:2), the woman at the well (see John 4:1–26), and the woman caught in the act of adultery (see John 8:1–11) became case histories to show her that God truly cares and fully forgives.

The stories of the prodigal son (see Luke 15:11–31) and the good Samaritan (see Luke 10:25–37) expressed to her the God who freely gives Himself and accepts us in repentance and consecration just as if we had never sinned.

It was a great moment for Beth when she made a commitment. She came to know God personally by internalizing the image of Christ as a model for her lifestyle.

Joy is not an elusive search for a vague idea called happiness. Joy is the sense of imperturbable gladness in spite of the circumstances.

Joy is a sense of self-worth that transcends the past by choosing the spiritual life over the secular and by experiencing the new self over the old self.

A single parent who found this to be true in his life shares his thoughts in the following letter:

> As you know, the past year has been very painful and difficult at times, but the joy of the Lord has been my strength.

When confronted with the reality of divorce for the second time, I wondered if I could make it back a second time—back to a state of wholeness and happiness; back to a state of emotional well-being.

When I returned home from a business trip and found my wife had moved out, my first reaction was rage. In the weeks and months that followed, I felt like I was riding on an emotional rollercoaster. Just when I'd get to the point where I was enjoying being single again and glad to be rid of "that selfish gold-brick," I'd take a nose-dive and find myself so overcome with grief I could barely function.

At the height of this adversity, there were days when I reached the end of myself and my resources. During these times, I learned the sustaining power of intercessory prayer as you and several others "stood the gap" before God in my behalf. In my darkest moments, I sensed your prayers and felt His unfailing love flood my soul and bring the strength to hang on despite the circumstances.

There were days when, in my greatest frustration, I gave in to anger, resentment, and self-pity. In your pastoral counseling, I found compassion, understanding, and forgiveness, plus a firm, but gentle, discipline and encouragement to rise above the circumstances. In trying to live out Matthew 6:33, I have experienced the power of prayer in the personal pursuit of righteousness in Christ Jesus; in short, I am getting to know God personally!

Oftentimes, the burden of single fatherhood has seemed more than I could bear. As I watched my seven-year-old daughter mourn the loss of a stepmother on the heels of losing her mother, I felt a tremendous sense of guilt and a basic inadequacy to continue on as both mother and father.

Through it all, I have learned to experience joy in the midst of sorrow and pain; my joy comes from the love of Jesus. As bad as some days have been, there have been more days when my heart has soared to new heights in the fellowship of the Holy Spirit and members of my church.

In Christ, no destruction is irreversible, no damage too severe, no hurt too deep, no pain too intense for the love of God to fail us. Adversity is really an opportunity for growth and maturity in Him; a time when, in our greatest hurt, we can experience His greatest assurance to know that "all things work together for good for those who love God, and are called according to His purpose" (Romans 8:28). It is in this blessed assurance that I have found unspeakable joy in the midst of unfathomable, personal loss.

What does this letter really say? In essence it shares with us five principles for sustaining joy.

1. Practice the sustaining power of intercessory prayer (see Rom. 8:26).
2. Anticipate strength to hang on despite the circumstances (see Eph. 6:13–18; 1 Cor. 10:1; 1 Pet. 5:10).
3. Pursue the righteousness of God in the personal knowledge of Jesus Christ (see Rom. 1:16,17; 2 Cor. 5:21; Phil. 3:9).
4. Renew strength through the experience of worship (see Isa. 40:31; 1 Pet. 5:7; Phil. 4:13).
5. Maintain support through the fellowship of believers (see Heb. 10:25; Rom. 12:13; 15:5; James 5:16).

This is the internalized image that allows us to sustain a healthy level of self-esteem and to keep our joy. "In Christ, no destruction is irreversible, no damage too severe, no hurt too deep, no pain too intense for the love of God to fail us."

6 *Stress Point*

Ambivalent Lifestyle

PLANNING YOUR PRIORITIES

Scriptural
Source
    Matthew 6:33,34

Joy
Sustainers
    Sense the times
Seek the timeless
Sort out the temporary
Sanctify the tomorrows

6

PLANNING YOUR PRIORITIES

Perhaps the most important and significant premise for joyful living is embodied in the statement, "All behavior is need motivated." What this means is that we order certain behavioral priorities to meet corresponding basic needs in our lives.

For instance, all of us have physical needs—the basic drives of hunger and thirst, together with the necessity of appropriate temperature, activity, and sexual fulfillment. We set priorities to meet those physical needs.

All of us have security needs—the desire for shelter, warmth, and freedom from fear and pain. We set priorities to meet those security needs.

All of us have esteem needs—the desire to feel worthwhile, valued, and of importance. We set priorities to meet those esteem needs.

All of us have belonging needs—the desire to feel accepted as a contributing member of a group. We set priorities to meet those belonging needs.

All of us have actualization needs—the desire to be significant, fulfilled, and challenged. We set priorities to meet those actualization needs.

The problem is that too often we get out of balance between our priorities and seek fulfillment that ultimately erodes our joyful living. Thus, when we talk about being "'out of sync,'" we are really referring to an acute or chronic condition of emotional ambivalence—a condition of inner conflict resulting from a discrepancy between personal priorities and the ability to gratify needs.

SENSE THE TIMES

The bottom-line reason for being out of balance is that we get caught up in the stress of the times. Regardless of our theology, we cannot ignore the diabolic dilemma of the day. We cannot ignore the evidence that an overriding spiritual battle is manifesting itself in the competition for nuclear power, political domination, and economic superiority. What we read about in our newspapers and view on our television sets are really battles of priorities.

Discernible signs of the times result from satanic influence, which bogs us down under stress and causes us to lose the presence of joy. The Bible is clear that today's negative influences are masterminded by a super spirit called Satan that slanders (see Job 1:9), attacks (see Job 2:7), opposes (see Zech. 3:1), tempts (see Matt. 4:1), disconnects (see Matt. 13:18,19), and confuses (see John 13:2). Thus, much of our time is spent dealing with pressures and forces that work against us to prevent us from having productive, joyful lives.

Sensing the times enables us to understand that joy is dependent on setting our priorities so that the positives—energized by the Spirit of Christ—counteract and control the negatives.

This was the strategy of the apostle Paul in Galatians 2:20, "I have been crucified with Christ; it is no longer I who live, but Christ lives in me; and the life which I now live in the flesh I live by faith in the Son of God, who loved me and gave Himself for me."

In fact, this is what the apostle John had in mind in 1 John 4:4 when he stated that "He who is in you is greater than he who is in the world," and Paul declared in Romans 16:20 that "the God of peace will crush Satan under your feet shortly."

Perhaps this strategy is best illustrated by the famous Winston Churchill, the first honorary citizen of the United States. On May 13, 1940, when England was facing the onslaught of Nazi Germany under Hitler, Prime Minister Churchill made a historic speech before the House of Commons in which he said,

> You ask, "what is our aim?" I can answer in one word: Victory—victory at all costs, victory in spite of all terror, victory however long and hard the road may be; for without victory there is no survival. I have nothing to offer but blood, toil, tears and sweat.

Two weeks later Churchill delivered the inspiring words that would weld England into an iron pillar:

> Even though large tracts of Europe in many old and famous states have fallen or may fall into the grip of the Gestapo, we shall not flag or fail. We shall go on to the end. We shall fight in France; we shall fight on the seas and oceans; we shall fight with growing confidence and growing strength in the air; we shall defend our island, whatever the cost may be. We shall fight on the beaches; we shall fight on the landing grounds; we shall fight in the fields and in the streets; we shall fight in the hills. We shall never surrender.

Churchill sensed the times, and his priority was very clear— "We shall never surrender." In a very real way this must be the priority of every person who wants to live a life of joy—never surrender to the negative signs of the times.

Well, we say, that sounds great! But how do we make it work? So often we feel like the little boy who entered an essay contest at school. Two weeks later he got his paper back, and when he went home from school, his mother noticed he looked perplexed. Recognizing the essay in his hand, she asked him, "How did you do in the contest?" In reply he said, "Well, I didn't win a prize; all I got was *horrible* mention."

Isn't that the way we read it? We are looking for the win, but sometimes all we get is *horrible* mention.

Talking about priorities is one thing; setting and keeping them is another. Perhaps we feel like the young evangelist who as a single college boy preached youth revivals and became famous for his sermon to parents, "Ten Commandments for Rearing Children."

After college he got married; two years later he and his wife were blessed with their first child. He vigorously preached the sermon until the baby was two years old. Then he changed the title to "Ten Rules for Rearing Children." When the child went to grammar school, he changed the title to "Ten Suggestions for Rearing Children." When his child got to junior high school, he changed the title to "Ten Helpful Hints for Rearing Children." When his child finally entered high school, he stopped preaching this sermon altogether.

It is one thing to *preach* joy as a priority; it is another to *live* joy as a priority.

But here is where Christ comes in. His message is a priority message of joy and is the main theme of His ministry to His disciples on the Sermon on the Mount. What we find in this message is a lesson in priorities for every generation, and it centers in the words of Matthew 6:33,34:

But seek first the kingdom of God and His righteousness, and all these things shall be added to you. Therefore do not worry about tomorrow, for tomorrow will worry about its own things. Sufficient for the day is its own trouble.

SEEK THE TIMELESS

But seek first the kingdom of God and His righteousness . . .

This is the first and highest priority of life—seeking the kingdom of God. *To seek* means "to pursue actively." It is to run after with diligence, to push to the limit, to give the highest place.

In this case the word *seek* means "to develop the highest that is in us." Luke 17:21 tells us that the kingdom of God is within us, and Romans 14:17 states that the kingdom of God is not eating and drinking, but righteousness and peace and joy in the Holy Spirit.

Thus, we are to live our lives in the constant development of the spiritual nature that reflects His righteousness, the righteousness of God. The word *righteousness,* as it is used in this passage, refers to accepting the claims of God and internalizing them as our own governing principles for everyday life.

This idea was driven home to me while conducting a seminar for business people interested in incorporating spiritual principles into business life. At the close of one of the sessions, I allowed some time for questions, answers, and discussion. The comments made by an older member of the group had a tremendous impact. In his words:

> There was a point in my life when I had one goal in mind— to make a million dollars. I was well on the way but came to the realization that I was losing my wife and children in the process.
> I was contemplating an affair; my wife was talking about divorce; my son had been arrested for a DUI; my daughter was experimenting with marijuana; we were all moving in different directions.

One Easter we made our annual pilgrimage to church, and the Resurrection message finally came alive in my heart. I called a family conference, and we made a covenant to try to live as a family by the Ten Commandments through the power of the resurrected Christ.

We instituted family devotions; conducted a family interpretation of the commandments; discussed our progress at every meal we were together.

To make a long story short, this new priority of life transformed us. I made the million dollars with my wife by my side. My son became a successful college professor and an active church elder. My daughter is married to a most responsible and loving man.

We owe it all to making the spiritual life our highest priority.

This is the basis for joy—the priority of the morality of God as interpreted in Christ and lived out in the timeless truths of the kingdom.

The timeless life is the moral life, and the moral life is the happy life. But what is morality, anyway? Morality begins with the law of God as outlined in the Ten Commandments (see Exod. 20:3–17).

1. You shall have no other gods before Me.
2. You shall not make for yourself any carved image.
3. You shall not take the name of the LORD your God in vain.
4. Remember the Sabbath day, to keep it holy.
5. Honor your father and your mother.
6. You shall not murder.
7. You shall not commit adultery.
8. You shall not steal.
9. You shall not bear false witness.
10. You shall not covet.

Commensurately, morality is centered in the life of Christ, and we hear Him say,

"And you shall love the LORD your God with all your heart, with all your soul, with all your mind, with all your strength." This is the first commandment. And the second, like it, is this: "You shall love your neighbor as yourself." There is no other commandment greater than these" (Mark 12:30,31).

Christ, in turn, interpreted the function of these commandments in terms of the spirit of the law rather than the letter of the law. For instance, He talked about murder in terms of anger and hate (see Matt. 5:21,22) and adultery in terms of lust and inordinate desire (see Matt. 5:27–30). Further, He made a big point of forgiveness (see Matt. 6:14,15) and modeled a lifestyle of servanthood (see Matt. 18:1–9) and compassion in His parables of the lost sheep, the lost coin, and the lost son (see Luke 15).

In contemporary life, however, we can discern the aftermath of having lived outside the law of God.

As we have ignored the first commandment, we have experienced a loss of fear and respect for God with a subsequent *disregard for authority* in all phases of living.

As we have ignored the second commandment, we have witnessed the *revival of pagan worship practices,* and religion has degenerated into a do-it-yourself kit.

As we have ignored the third commandment, our agreements have lost substance; our *language has become base;* four-letter words are the order of the day.

As we have ignored the fourth commandment, we have *robbed God of glory* and made profit king with commerce as Sunday religion.

As we have ignored the fifth commandment, children have learned to disobey their parents with a resulting *loss of respect* for teachers, law enforcement officers, and general authority figures. Teenage crime is at an all-time high, and the social order is plagued by violence, riots, terrorism, and anarchy.

As we have ignored the sixth commandment, our penal institutions are overflowing; human *life has become cheap;* murder is the prime theme of the media.

As we have ignored the seventh commandment, over a million teenage pregnancies occur each year, venereal disease is rampant, and the *very fiber of the family has been weakened* to the extent that only 13 percent of households represent traditional family roles.

As we have ignored the eighth commandment, burglary has increased 200 percent in the past ten years; we have been forced to learn the art of self-defense; personal *property rights are constantly threatened,* and the security business is the booming investment of the decade.

As we have ignored the ninth commandment, *contracts have lost validity,* agreements are frequently ignored, and only in rare cases is a man's word his bond.

As we have ignored the tenth commandment, *greed has replaced responsibility;* the big rip-off is an accepted way of life; and fraud and deceit are too often tolerated as a necessary part of the business scene.

We *must* seek the timeless.

SORT OUT THE TEMPORARY

. . . and all these things shall be added to you.

Once we have given spiritual priority to the commandments, it then becomes necessary for us to sort out the temporary influences that hamper our joy. We have to live in the world, but as Christ prayed in John 17, we are in the world but not of the world (see John 17:15,16).

In this regard we are called upon to make choices as to how we are going to relate to the world and its temporary influences. We can *withdraw* into the ascetic life, but then we have to confront the

Great Commission to go into all the world and make disciples (see Matt. 28:19). We can *rise above* the world and say like the Pharisee, "God, I thank you that I am not like other men" (Luke 18:11), but then we have to confront the words of Jesus in Matthew 5:20, "Unless your righteousness exceeds the righteousness of the scribes and Pharisees, you will by no means enter the kingdom of heaven." We can conflict with the world and constantly be in a state of *tension and judgment,* but then we have to confront John 3:16, "For God so loved the world that He gave His only begotten Son, that whoever believes in Him should not perish." We can *accommodate* the world until we are so much like the world that there are no differentiations or distinctions, but then we have to confront the command, "Do not love the world or the things in the world. If anyone loves the world, the love of the Father is not in him" (1 John 2:15).

There is a better way! The way of Christ is *to redeem the world.* We are to be the light of the world; the salt of the earth; the city that is set upon a hill that cannot be hidden (see Matt. 5:13,14); the leaven that leavens the whole lump (Gal. 5:9).

We are to sort out the temporary. In our day we have been bombarded with a persistent, secularistic humanism that calls for us to develop our own abilities, determine our own destiny, live by our own reasoning, reject authoritarian controls and cultivate our personal sense of morality. In short, secularistic humanism emphasizes the temporary with little regard for the timeless.

According to Tim LaHaye, humanism elevates the wisdom of man over the wisdom of God and establishes the premise that

man is basically good. His goals should be self-actualization, self-determination and self-indulgence. Since there is no life after death, it is in man's best interest to find the "good life" here and now. "Do your own thing"; stress human rights; be lenient to criminals.[1]

From this major premise the *Humanist Manifesto* has been devised, which incorporates five major tenets: (1) *Atheism:* ". . . as nontheists we begin with man not God . . ."; (2) *Evolution:* ". . . The human species is an emergence from natural evolutionary forces . . ."; (3) *Amorality:* ". . . ethics is autonomous and situational . . . stems from self-interest . . ."; (4) *Self-Autonomy:* ". . . we believe in maximum individual autonomy—reject all religious, moral codes that suppress freedom . . ."; (5) *Socialist One World View:* ". . . we have reached a turning point in human history where the best often is to transcend the limits of national sovereignty and move toward the building of a world community . . . the peaceful adjudication of difference by international courts."[2]

But what happens when we trust in temporary resources and mortal men? For one thing, *we deny the supernatural*. In the nineteenth century, the philosopher Auguste Comte grew weary of theological abstractions and subtleties, and he tried to find a way forward by denying the reality of the supernatural. Recognizing that worship was important, he sought to establish a religion of humanity and built elaborate and beautiful buildings in which to conduct colorful ritual and pageantry. The attempt was unsuccessful. When people came to worship, there was no God present to praise and adore. It became an exercise in self-interest and narcissistic indulgence.

For another thing, *we negate the efficacy of worship*. In the twentieth century, humanists have conducted similar experiments and have denied both God and the necessity of worship. Although humanists have preached a pure ethic and have contributed heavily to social service, they have laughed at the Ten Commandments, sneered at the New Testament beatitudes, ridiculed the Sunday worship services, and prided themselves that they have entered into a self-made liberty. The humanistic experiment hasn't worked, however. The promised utopia and its socially engineered population have degenerated into a world of violence dominated by a spirit of rebellion and greed.

There is only one step from the worship of man to the worship of the state and open idolatry. Human rulers have no authority and can develop no policy capable of demanding the total allegiance of their subjects, and the mere assumption of such authority ultimately leads into slavery.

The only answer to the spirit of the age is our persistent trust in the God of Abraham, Isaac, and Jacob. We can reach this conclusion because the Lord remains faithful forever. We need to take a timeless approach to life in both our secular pursuits and our spiritual concerns. Here is our code of beliefs by which we sort out the temporary: (1) *God:* Genesis 1:1, "In the beginning God . . ."; (2) *Divine Creation:* Genesis 1:27, ". . . God created man in His own image . . ."; (3) *Moral Responsibility:* Luke 11:28, ". . . blessed are those who hear the word of God and keep it!"; (4) *Servants of God:* 1 Corinthians 6:19,20, ". . . your body is the temple of the Holy Spirit who is in you . . . and you are not your own . . . you were bought at a price; therefore glorify God in your body and in your spirit, which are God's"; (5) *Eternal View of World:* John 14:2,3, "In My Father's house are many mansions; if it were not so, I would have told you. I go to prepare a place for you. And if I go and prepare a place for you, I will come again and receive you to Myself; that where I am, there you may be also."

SANCTIFY THE TOMORROWS

Therefore do not worry about tomorrow, for tomorrow will worry about its own things. Sufficient for the day is its own trouble.

"Don't worry!" Christ said. When we lose our joy, we worry. What is worry, anyway?

The experts tell us that worry is a low-grade fear. It is a chain of thoughts or mental images that are generally negative and all-consuming. In most instances, worry precedes a sense of prolonged stress to the point of distraction.

The Gypsies used to say that a "sad person is a sick person and the sickness is caused by worry." The Greeks described worry as opposing forces at work to tear a person apart. The Anglo-Saxons pictured worry like a vicious animal clutching at a person's throat.

Regardless of how we define it, we know that when we worry, we feel helpless and hapless. We have a sense of being inadequate and inefficient. We are harassed, tormented, and plagued until we are confused and frustrated. We don't know what decisions to make. We are not sure of what alternatives to choose. We don't have the right answers, and we aren't sure of the right questions.

The result is that our whole body reacts in a state of alarm. Our heartbeat accelerates; our pulse pounds; our blood vessels constrict; our muscles contract; the pituitary and adrenal glands secrete fluids that put us on edge.

In this regard, statistical experience tells us that 85 percent of the things we worry about never happen, and in most cases the 15 percent is not worth worrying about in the beginning. Christ knew this, and that is why He told His disciples in Matthew 6:25–27,

> Do not worry about your life, what you will eat or what you will drink; nor about your body, what you will put on. Is not life more than food and the body more than clothing? Look at the birds of the air, for they neither sow nor reap nor gather into barns; yet your heavenly Father feeds them. Are you not of more value than they? Which of you by worrying can add a single cubit to his stature?

The key here is sanctification. *To sanctify* means "to set apart and make holy." It is to consecrate and prepare for service. What this passage says is that as we sanctify our tomorrows we deal with the *precious present*. All we have is the now, and this now is to be lived out according to the highest priorities given to us by God in the fulfillment of the self. We are to allow tomorrow to take care of itself or, in other words, to commit the future into the hands of a loving God.

This idea of sanctifying tomorrow was brought to me by a man who was dying with cancer. Throughout the whole ordeal of his sickness, he seemed to maintain a sense of enthusiasm and strength that was astounding. Time and time again he came near death, but each time he would rally, to the amazement of doctors, nurses, family, and friends.

On one occasion I was called to the hospital because death was imminent. When I arrived, he was in a coma, and we all thought it was the end. But once again he endured and was able to return home.

During this period, I asked him, "How are you able to survive these close bouts with death? What is your secret?" In answer he said:

> When it became certain that I had an inoperable cancer, I made a deal with the Lord.
> First, I promised to live every moment of my life like it was the only moment I would have.
> Second, I sanctified all my tomorrows and put them in the Lord's hands for whatever He had planned.
> Third, I pray every day for a miracle of healing but know that I've got a good deal either way. If I receive a miracle, it will be a tremendous testimony to the world of God's great power and grace. If I die, I will go home to be with the Lord, and in reality that will be an even better deal.
> Whether I live or die, I can't lose!

Joy is maintained by the way we plan our priorities. We cannot afford to have an ambivalent lifestyle. We are called upon to sense the times, seek the timeless, sort out the temporary, and sanctify the tomorrows. Whether we live or die, we can't lose!

7 *Stress Point*

The Pressure of Perversion

DISCIPLINING YOUR DESIRES

Scriptural
Source

Colossians 3:1–17

Joy
Sustainers

Make a definitive decision
Assume a distinctive determination
Seek a demonstrated development

7

DISCIPLINING YOUR DESIRES

It has been said that these are the best of times and the worst of times.

On the one hand, the best of times speaks of an unprecedented era of scientific, electronic, and technological achievement. On the other hand, the worst of times speaks of terrorism, hijackings, nuclear accidents, and social problems such as abortion, drug addiction, alcoholism, divorce, adultery, pornography, AIDS, and the scourge of battered wives and abused children.

No wonder Bob Hope, in one of his serious moments, made the statement, "This is a pressure-cooker world." No wonder Carl Jung, the Swiss psychologist, made the observation, "The central neurosis of our times is meaninglessness, and human nature simply can't stand emptiness and meaninglessness. It gets jumpy and jittery. It goes to pieces."

We look at our world, and there seems to be one overriding question: How do we discipline our desires? We are all created with basic desires essential for living, but when these desires are unrestrained and out of focus, we lose our joy. When our desires are uncontrolled, we are uncontrolled. When our desires are undisciplined, we are undisciplined. When our desires are uninhibited, we are uninhibited.

The apostle Paul was addressing this problem when he wrote the book of Colossians. The church had been infected by a virus known as Judaistic Gnosticism, which represented the worst of both the Greek and the Hebrew worlds. *Philosophically,* the idea was that salvation could be obtained only through knowledge, which negated Christ's power to be effective. *Theologically,* matter itself was considered to be evil, and the world was supposedly created by a series of angelic emanations. Faith was considered useless because belief without materialistic proof was null and void. *Behaviorally,* the goal of living was either asceticism—avoiding all the joys and pleasures of life through abuse of the body for the spirit's sake—or licentiousness—unrestrained carnality and a lifestyle of If it feels good, do it.

Paul's concern was that the problem of disciplining our desires could not be solved through legalistic means. The problem was much deeper and the solution more complex than restraint through rules and regulations.

This is what Paul had in mind in Colossians 2:23 when he said, "These things indeed have an appearance of wisdom in self-imposed religion, false humility, and neglect of the body, but are of no value against the indulgence of the flesh."

Here the essential word for flesh is the Greek word *sarx.* The flesh is the culprit in the process of disciplining our desires in order to live the life of joy.

The word *flesh* has multidimensional meanings. *Physically,* the word refers to the actual material property of the body—blood, sinews, skin, tissue, and chemical elements. *Scripturally,* the word is used to refer to mankind in general (see Joel 2:28ff.) and to describe the incarnation of Christ (see John 1:14).

Emotionally, the word is used to refer to the predisposition of the human nature to sin (see Rom. 3:23). *Intellectually,* the word describes the tendencies of the thought process in terms of lust, perversion, and immorality. As Jeremiah 17:9 puts it, "The heart is deceitful above all things, / And desperately wicked; / Who can know it?"

This is the discipline factor—bringing the flesh (the predisposition to sin and the tendency to think evil) under the Spirit's control. Paul told us that to be carnally minded is death but to be spiritually minded is life and peace (see Rom. 8:6). In Galatians 5:24 he stated, "Those who are Christ's have crucified the flesh with its passions and desires."

Here is the joy formula: Crucify the sinful nature with its passions and desires or, to put it in the vernacular, discipline our desires.

Immediately, however, when we read such a formula and pursue such a concept, we are prone to wonder, How is such a discipline possible?

The beautiful thing about the Bible is that it never states a principle without giving a methodology. Therefore, we can turn to Colossians 3 and see what we need to do to discipline our desires.

DISCIPLINE DEMANDS
A DEFINITIVE DECISION

Decide! Decide! This is the starting point. Paul put it this way,

If then you were raised with Christ, seek those things which are above, where Christ is, sitting at the right hand of God. Set your mind on things above, not on things on the earth. For you died, and your life is hidden with Christ in God. When Christ who is our life appears, then you also will appear with Him in glory (Col. 3:1,2).

We are what we choose, and behavior is the result of choice. Thus, we are responsible for our behavior, but thankfully, we can change behavior.

We maintain joy by changing those behaviors that bring us

sorrow, sadness, and difficulty. We make an intellectual-emotional-spiritual decision to function in a way that brings the highest productivity to our lives. We set our hearts on things above . . . we set our minds on things above . . . we die to the old life . . . we hide in Christ . . . we appear with Him in glory.

In essence, *joy is the result of self-control*. Cain murdered his brother Abel—the lack of self-control. Moses lost his temper, and he never set foot in the Promised Land—the lack of self-control. David not only had an affair with Bathsheba but arranged for the death of her husband—the lack of self-control. Samson revealed the secret of his power to Delilah, and it cost him his power with God—the lack of self-control. Judas betrayed Jesus for thirty pieces of silver and grieved himself to suicide—the lack of self-control.

What about us? Don't we have to deal with the hate of a Cain? the lost temper of a Moses? the lust of a David? the carelessness of a Samson? the hypocrisy of a Judas? The Bible says if we really want joy, we must learn to discipline our desires through the power of self-control.

Self-control comes from choice. This is the message of Deuteronomy 30:19, "Choose life, that both you and your descendants may live." This is the message of Joshua 24:15, "But as for me and my house, we will serve the LORD." This is the message of the apostle Paul, "But God forbid that I should boast except in the cross of our Lord Jesus Christ, by whom the world has been crucified to me, and I to the world" (Gal. 6:14).

And this is the message of Jim, a college basketball player who called me on the phone and in a triumphant voice said, "I have just experienced the greatest victory of my life."

Jim is a Christian who went from a small town to a large university as a celebrated football player. As often happens, he got caught up in the party life and soon found himself indulging in behavior that was not in keeping with his Christian values.

One night he and his friends got high. The suggestion was made to rob an all-night liquor store—just on a "lark" and for the "excitement." "Suddenly," Jim said, "I got cold sober. It was like a light went on inside of me and said, *You are risking your entire life on a very dumb move.* All of a sudden I got bold and made one of the world's great testimonies of the grace of God in my life and how I was missing the mark. I couldn't believe what I was saying. I sounded like you sound on Sunday morning."

By his own admission, Jim took a lot of verbal persecution that night, but he refused to go. The others did their thing. The proprietor was beaten up when he resisted. The offenders were apprehended, fined, expelled from school, and given a year of legal probation.

"I made a choice to discipline myself," Jim said, "and from now on I plan to live in Colossians 3."

This is how we keep our joy. We make a definitive decision to live by things above.

DISCIPLINE DEMANDS A DISTINCTIVE DETERMINATION

Decision is the start, but determination is the process. Paul emphasized this in Colossians 3:5-11 when he called for a distinctive break with the evil nature that energizes the world system.

First, he called for a *funeral:* "Therefore put to death your members which are on earth: fornication, uncleanness, passion, evil desire, and covetousness, which is idolatry. . . . put off all these: anger, wrath, malice, blasphemy, filthy language out of your mouth" (vv. 5,8).

Second, he called for a *resurrection:* "put on the new man who is renewed in knowledge according to the image of Him who created him" (v. 10).

The key to determination is a sense of inner directedness that does not yield to the pressures of the age—that identifies with the highest rather than the lowest, the best rather than the worst, the ideal rather than the average, the excellent rather than the mediocre.

The man of the Bible who best exemplifies a distinctive determination is Moses. He was born of godly parents in a time of persecution when the Egyptian Pharaoh had ordered the death of all male Hebrew babies. To save his life, Moses' parents hid him for three months and then, when he was no longer safe in his hiding place, set him afloat in a basket on the Nile River.

After being discovered and taken in by Pharaoh's daughter, he was nursed by his own mother. Miriam, his sister, had persuaded Pharaoh's daughter to allow her to secure a Hebrew nurse to care for and rear the baby Moses.

Moses grew up in Pharaoh's court and probably was looked upon as the heir apparent to the throne. However, at age forty he had to flee Egypt because he murdered an Egyptian for beating a Hebrew slave. He found refuge in the land of Midian and married Zipporah, the daughter of Jethro, a shepherd.

Moses settled down and lived the nomadic life of a sheepherder for the next forty years until he received a divine call from God through the burning bush experience (see Exod. 3). Obeying this supernatural commission, he returned to Egypt to deliver the people of Israel from bondage.

From all human standpoints, Moses was a poor choice and evidently had a poor self-image. His arguments to God were I have no ability (see Exod. 3:11); I have no message (see 3:13); I have no authority (see Exod. 4:1); I have no eloquence (see 4:10); I have no inclination—I don't want to go (see 4:13).

From God's standpoint, however, Moses was a determined

man, and he was assured by God that he would have God's divine presence (see Exod. 3:12); God's divine authority (see 3:13,14); God's divine help (see Exod. 4:2–8); and the cooperation of Aaron to go with him and help him in the mission (see 4:14–16).

It was determination that God saw in Moses, and it was Moses' determined spirit that took him through the Egyptian plagues, the Red Sea experience, the wilderness wanderings, the people's stubbornness under duress, the rebellion and disobedience represented by the golden calf at Sinai, and his own limitation. In spite of it all, Moses never gave up.

In fact, Deuteronomy 34:10–12 tells us:

> But since then there has not arisen in Israel a prophet like Moses, whom the LORD knew face to face, in all the signs and wonders which the LORD sent him to do in the land of Egypt, before Pharaoh, before all his servants, and in all his land, and by all that mighty power and all the great terror which Moses performed in the sight of all Israel.

Joy comes from the distinctive determination not to give in, which is what the apostle Paul modeled in Philippians 1:27:

> Only let your conduct be worthy of the gospel of Christ, so that whether I come and see you or am absent, I may hear of your affairs, that you stand fast in one spirit, with one mind striving together for the faith of the gospel.

This kind of determination is best illustrated by the message of the movie *Chariots of Fire* in which Eric Liddell was the central character. Eric was a man who lived forcefully by his convictions. Because he would not run in the Olympics on Sunday, he entered a different race, and he won a gold medal in the Olympics of 1924.

Liddell was called to be a missionary to China and became a

teacher at the Anglo-Chinese College in Tientsin in order to fulfill that calling. After teaching there for a period of time, he went into the interior and traveled from village to village on foot and by bicycle spreading the good news of the gospel over hundreds of thousands of miles.

World War II broke out, and the Japanese invaded China. Liddell was branded, along with many others of Western heritage, as an "enemy national," and in 1943 he was confined in a prison camp one hundred fifty yards by two hundred yards with a thousand other so-called nationalist enemies. While he was there, his determined life had an impact on the prison camp. He organized athletic events, conducted worship services, preached the gospel (to which many responded in faith), counseled with people, and comforted the sick and the dying.

His determined influence is reflected in the writings of a man named David Michell who was a child in the camp during that time. Michell writes: "None of us will ever forget this man who was totally committed to putting God first, a man whose humble life combined muscular Christianity with radiant godliness."[1]

Finally, in 1945, Eric Liddell died of a brain tumor in that prison camp.

Liddell's story gives us insight into the meaning of determination, and Liddell has articulated that determination in a Christian manual that gives four tests of the moral law by which we are to measure ourselves:

(1) *Am I truthful?* Are there any conditions under which I will tell a lie? Can I be depended on to tell the truth no matter what the cost?

(2) *Am I honest?* Can I be trusted in money matters? In my work, even when no one is looking? With other people's reputations? With myself—or do I rationalize and become self-defensive?

(3) *Am I pure?* In my habit? In my thought life? In my motives? In my relations with the opposite sex?

(4) *Am I selfish?* In the demands I make on my family, spouse, or associates? Am I badly balanced, full of moods—cold today and warm tomorrow? Do I indulge in nerves that spoil my happiness and that of those around me? Am I unrestrained in my pleasures, the kind I enjoy without considering the effect they have on my soul? Am I unrestrained in my work, refusing to take reasonable rest and exercise? Am I unrestrained in small self-indulgences, letting myself become the slave of habits, however harmless they may appear to me? Let us put ourselves before ourselves and look at ourselves.[2]

The determined life reaches for the deepest resources in Christ. Determination stands up and says, I'm taking charge of my life. I'm taking charge of my schedule. I'm taking charge of my attitudes. I'm taking charge of my responses. I'm taking charge of my behavior.

It says in effect, I'm not going to bend to the temptations of the world. I'm not going to give in to the frustrations of the day. I refuse to be immobilized by the lower nature and the works of the flesh. "I know whom I have believed and am persuaded that He is able to keep what I have committed to Him until that Day" (2 Tim. 1:12).

DISCIPLINE DEMANDS
A DEMONSTRATED DEVELOPMENT

Discipline starts with decision, is sustained by determination, but succeeds in development. As Paul put it in Colossians 3:15–17,

And let the peace of God rule in your hearts, to which also you were called in one body; and be thankful. Let the word of Christ dwell in you richly in all wisdom, teaching and admonishing one another in psalms and hymns and spiritual songs, singing with grace in your hearts to the Lord. And whatever you do in word or deed, do all in the name of the Lord Jesus, giving thanks to God the Father through Him.

Within this context the result of disciplining our desires should be a lifestyle characterized by the rule of God's peace and the indwelling of God's Word.

In the Old Testament, the English word *peace* is derived from the Hebrew word *shalom* and is defined as "a sense of wholeness, well-being, and prosperity." In the New Testament, *peace* is derived from the Greek word *ĕirēnē* and is defined as "a sense of balance, completeness, and symmetry." In the vernacular it means having our act together and operating our lives in the completeness of Christ, regardless of the circumstances. With this peace at the center we are able to maintain a lifestyle that truly functions in the name of Jesus Christ.

Obviously, there is a need for a revival of the Word lifestyle, but how are we to do everything in the name of Jesus Christ? How are we to demonstrate our development in the discipline of our desires?

Based on the authority of God's Word and its intrinsic value, the following statements give us a broad framework for moral Christian behavior:

Moral actions, decisions, and attitudes produce
1. The capacity to internalize faith.
2. The strength of integrity in relationships.
3. The appreciation of human dignity and worth.
4. The acceptance of freedom in responsibility to God and the Christian community.
5. The attitudes of love and creative cooperation.
6. The fulfillment of capability.
7. The development of absolute convictions.

Immoral actions, decisions, and attitudes produce
1. The capacity to manipulate and deceive.
2. The weakness of dishonesty and fraud.
3. The degradation of human dignity and worth.
4. The promotion of freedom of the self at the expense of God and the community in exploitive behavior.
5. The attitudes of disrespect and rebellion.
6. The failure to fulfill capability.
7. The lapse into relativism in which the end justifies the means.[3]

Although this list is not exhaustive, it does provide a value framework in which decisions can be made for the creation of trust, confidence, and integrity in relationship to God and our fellow beings. Behavior that causes deceit and duplicity, creates mistrust and misunderstanding, builds barriers, destroys friendships, violates faith, and breaks down communication and cooperation is *immoral* behavior.

The proof of our behavior is in the morality we demonstrate. Perhaps this point is best summarized in the experience of a Jewish family illustrated in the book *Betrayed*.

The daughter went away to college and became a Christian through the witnessing of her friends. She shared with her family what had happened, but her conversion devastated her Jewish father, mother, and sister.

In rebuttal, her father set out to disprove that Jesus Christ was the Messiah. He took off ninety days from his business and researched historical documents from the Jewish viewpoint as contrasted with the Christian perspective.

As he was working through the maze of materials, the one thing that continually touched him, impressed him, and haunted him the most was the peace manifested in his daughter's life. Without a doubt there was a tremendous change in her demeanor and personal bearing.

She appeared to have peace in her heart and a brightness in her soul. She radiated a sense of well-being that he and the other family members could not understand.

In his search he finally came to the conclusion that there had to be something to that peace, and he wanted it. As he was going through the Word, it finally struck his heart that Jesus Christ is the source and center of peace and that He must be the Messiah in order to bring that kind of peace to life.

Ultimately, he accepted Christ, and his wife and other daughter did, too. They have since established a church for Jewish believers in New York and are making known to the world that it is true—Jesus Christ is peace.[4]

This is how we keep our joy and relieve the pressure of perversion. We discipline our desires through a definitive decision, a distinctive determination, and a demonstrated development as outlined in Colossians 3:1-17.

8 *Stress Point*

The Pain of Emptiness

FOCUSING YOUR FAITH

Scriptural Source   Hebrews 12:1-3

Joy Sustainers   Draw from history
Travel light
Set a secure course
Hang tough

8

FOCUSING YOUR FAITH

It was miserable, rainy, and cold. Brenda looked out the large picture window of my third-story office and said in morose tones, "If I had my way, I would dive headfirst through this window and solve all my problems with suicide."

I responded, "Sometimes we all feel overwhelmed and would like to escape from it all, but then we recognize that we have to live, and maybe there are other choices that would make life really worth living."

In reply, she said, "What alternatives? I have it all. I have money, prestige, health, and every opportunity any person could possibly want. Yet, my life seems meaningless and miserable. My husband is a workaholic; my children are in college; my friends bore me to tears, and if I have to play another hand of bridge, I will literally scream."

After we explored her feelings about her emptiness, it became apparent that her faith was out of focus. She had all her material needs met and was blessed with golden opportunities, but somewhere along the line she had never truly focused her faith. Consequently, she had no joy.

THE HYPE

Too often we are caught up in media hype and believe that if we follow all of the secular prescriptions, our lives will be filled with joy and happiness.

We try the leading brands, use the right commodities, wear the latest fashions, and follow the available self-help procedures; yet, the battle of emptiness persists.

The popular hype is as our self-image goes, so goes our happiness. But the truth is that as our faith increases, so does our happiness. Self-image is important; a positive outlook on life is necessary; but neither a strong self-image nor a healthy worldview is complete without a focused faith.

THE FOCUS

When our faith is out of focus, we start groping to meet the pressures of life. Sometimes we vacillate between being shy or aggressive. We may be easily hurt by criticism and may find ourselves steering away from close relationships. When our faith is out of focus, we tend to play games with ourselves and others. We are prone to hide our true selves and wear a well-adjusted mask. We struggle with being overly defensive, and we blame our mistakes and shortcomings on others.

When our faith is out of focus, we tend to become suspicious of change. We avoid new experiences and seem to take a certain inner delight in the failure of others.

When our faith is *in* focus, however, we are able to accept constructive criticism and handle unjust blame with poise and appropriate emotional response. As a result, we find ourselves at ease in meeting new people, and we are able to enjoy and value close relationships.

When our faith is *in* focus, we can be honest and open about our feelings. We can even laugh about our mistakes as we attempt to learn and profit from them.

When our faith is *in* focus, we welcome new challenges to tackle. We come to a healthy appraisal of ourselves that enables us to give ourselves credit when credit is due.

When our faith is *in* focus, we enjoy life to its fullest. We can enter into the happiness of others as they succeed and achieve personal goals and dreams.

Having our faith *in* focus is the meaning of biblical faith—it is trusting God so that we can make the most out of every situation.

This is the message of Hebrews 11:1, "Now faith is the substance of things hoped for, and the evidence of things not seen."

This is the message of Hebrews 11:6, "But without faith it is impossible to please Him, for he who comes to God must believe that He is, and that He is a rewarder of those who diligently seek Him."

This is what the apostle John was driving at when he declared, "For whatever is born of God overcomes the world. And this is the victory that has overcome the world—our faith" (1 John 5:4).

We have not been made to live in the hype of doubt, fear, worry, and low self-esteem. Rather, we have been made to live in trust, and trust is the principle that sustains an attitude of joy in every circumstance of life.

Proverb 3:5,6 tells us: "Trust in the LORD with all your heart, / And lean not on your own understanding; / In all your ways acknowledge Him, / And He shall direct your paths."

Isaiah 50:10 encourages us by saying, "Who walks in darkness / And has no light? / Let him trust in the name of the LORD / And rely on his God."

When we trust the Lord and rely on Him, we have our faith properly focused.

THE SOURCE

Faith should be the source of every response we make in life. If that is to happen, however, faith has to become more than wishful thinking on our part. Far too often we view faith as some kind of never-never land fantasy that operates as our own personal genie to bring instant health, wealth, and total happiness.

Within this framework the story is told of three ministers shipwrecked on a remote desert island. One was a priest; one was a rabbi; one was a charismatic preacher.

In order to make the most efficient use of their time and talent, the priest was designated to do the cooking, since he had more experience living alone and caring for himself. The rabbi, because of his disciplined lifestyle as an Orthodox Jew, was chosen to sit on the beach and watch for ships or planes to signal for help. The charismatic—because of his need to be on the move—was designated to gather wood and hunt for food and supplies as well as keep up general morale through constant praise, worship, and general enthusiasm.

One day a huge bottle washed up on the shore. The rabbi pulled it out of the water and called for his two colleagues to share his discovery.

In anticipation they pulled out the cork and watched in awe as a giant-sized genie was released from thousands of years of captivity. In deep gratitude the genie said, "I have the power to grant three wishes to anyone I want whenever I want. Because you have rescued me from this prison, I will grant each of you the wish of your life—regardless!"

Since the rabbi was the spotter of the bottle, he was given the first wish and, after he thought about it, said, "All my life I've wanted to visit Jerusalem and pray at the Wailing Wall. My wish is that I might go to the Wailing Wall of the temple in Jerusalem." Poof! Just like that it happened, and the rabbi was gone.

The priest was second and said, "If my calendar calculations are correct, Notre Dame is playing Southern California this afternoon, and I haven't missed a Notre Dame–Southern California game in ten years. My wish is to attend that game today." Poof! Just like that he was gone.

Then came the charismatic preacher who, in deep sincerity, said, "You know, I have really learned to love and appreciate that priest and rabbi. They have become just like my own brothers, and I wish they were here with me right now."

Isn't that the way it happens to us sometimes? We confuse faith with wishful thinking. We have to see faith as more than some kind of organized emotional decree that directs God to do our personal bidding. Sometimes we feel that through some structured, legalistic approach, God will be obligated to fulfill our every whim and desire.

Tony had this problem. As we talked, he pulled out a "faith book" that had all sorts of structured prayers, elaborate formulas guaranteed to bring instantaneous results if followed to the letter.

He said, "I've done all these things diligently for months, and all I have achieved is a chronic headache and a confused mind. Things are getting worse rather than better, and I'm beginning to wonder if this faith jazz is really what it is cracked up to be."

As I looked over Tony's book, I remembered a periodical that featured some government agency questions asked on various official forms.

For instance, on one United Nations' questionnaire there is the statement, "If your answer to the above question is 'Yes,' please explain 'Why not?'"

On a questionnaire for the Army Counterintelligence Corps there is the question, "Have you or any of your relatives ever committed suicide?"

In a description of the physical requirements for a civil service job at the U.S. Naval Air Station in Quonset Point, Rhode Island, it is stated that one must have the "ability to distinguish basic colors without the use of a hearing aid."

To approach faith as a regulated procedure that binds God and puts Him in a box is to miss the point and negate the source.

What is faith, then? How does it operate?

To find an answer, we can go to the book of Hebrews, a source that helps us make faith a workable reality.

Hebrews is the faith book and centers on the covenantal relationship we have with Christ, who is the fulfillment of the Old Testament legalistic system, religious rituals, and ceremonial worship. In this regard Hebrews 8:5,6 tells us that the Old Testament priesthood and prototypes "serve the copy and shadow of the heavenly things. . . . But now He has obtained a more excellent ministry, inasmuch as He is also mediator of a better covenant, which was established on better promises."

This is why Hebrews is often called the fifth gospel. The four gospels focus on what Christ did on earth, and Hebrews centers on what Christ is doing now in heaven.

So, how do we focus our faith in a way that keeps our joy?

A JOYOUS FAITH IS FOCUSED ON THE PERSON AND WORK OF JESUS CHRIST

First, according to Hebrews 12:2, faith that works has to be focused on the very person of Christ. The writer admonishes us to look "unto Jesus, the author and finisher of our faith, who for the joy that was set before Him endured the cross, despising the shame, and has sat down at the right hand of the throne of God." Further, verse 3 tells us to "consider Him who endured such hostility from sinners against Himself, lest you become weary and discouraged in your souls."

What this means is that our joy is not based on our own abilities, talents, or personal adjustment to life; rather, it is focused on the fact that we can do all things through Christ who strengthens us (see Phil. 4:13).

In a contemporary sense, this was the gist of a letter I received from a man in New Mexico. One day while traveling the I-75 freeway, which passes our church, he saw all the cars parked during the morning worship hours. He impulsively pulled off the freeway and decided to join us after not having darkened a church door for some eight years.

In his words:

> I attended your services on Sunday with a heavy heart and no hope for a marriage that was on the rocks. My wife, a native of Georgia, left me in New Mexico because of my drinking, unfaithfulness, and general lifestyle in the fast lane. She returned to live with her parents while we settled things.
>
> Since I had to be in Atlanta, I talked her into spending some time with me on a Sunday. While on my way to see her, I passed your church, was fascinated by all the cars parked in every conceivable direction, and stopped to see what was going on.
>
> It was a Communion Sunday, and I was deeply moved by the worship of the people to the point I asked Christ to come into my heart after eight years of not having attended a church anywhere. As a boy I made a profession of faith, but after college it was really a thing of the past.
>
> When I met my wife that afternoon I shared my experience, and it was the beginning of a reconciliation. I returned to New Mexico, found a church, and have been growing in the faith of Jesus Christ ever since.
>
> It took a year, but my home is now united and my two children have a stable family situation with Christ at the head and two people who have renewed a covenantal relationship with Him and each other.

This man learned that joy comes from a focused faith in the person and work of Jesus Christ.

A JOYOUS FAITH IS FOCUSED ON THE POWER TO HANDLE PRESSURE

Therefore we also, since we are surrounded by so great a cloud of witnesses, let us lay aside every weight, and the sin which so easily ensnares us, and let us run with endurance the race that is set before us (Heb. 12:1).

Second, joy is maintained when we focus our faith on the spiritual power available to handle the pressures of life. In this regard Hebrews 12:1 provides a formula for keeping joy—regardless!

Step One: Draw from History!

Therefore we also, since we are surrounded by so great a cloud of witnesses . . . Remember the great cloud of witnesses. We are not the first people who have had to undergo stress. We tend to get bogged down in the constant attention focused on stress and its negative effects, but now there is increasing evidence that not all stress is harmful. Indeed, stress can be a motivator to a more productive and fulfilling existence. As Dr. Sidney Lecker states, "Stress is essential for meeting challenges. If you didn't have it, you'd be dead."[1]

Certainly, this is the case of the gallery of role models described in Hebrews 11. Through faith these people "subdued kingdoms, worked righteousness, obtained promises, stopped the mouths of lions, quenched the violence of fire, escaped the edge of the sword." And because they had the power to turn weakness into strength and survive all types of persecution and hardship, they were commended for their faith (see Heb. 11:32–40).

Step Two: Travel Light!

 . . . *let us lay aside every weight, and the sin which so easily ensnares us* . . . Isn't it true that too many of us are weighted down with making payments, meeting deadlines, and trying to keep up with the Joneses? We travel too heavily packed.

It is appropriate and right to gain all we can, save all we can, and give all we can for the highest good. However, what value is there in having all the elements of the American dream and setting materialistic goals if it means broken homes, absentee fathers, divided-interest mothers, and fast-paced schedules? By focusing our lives like this, we are destined to hassle with overextended budgets and the constant quest for things and thrills.

As a leading architect once expressed to me,

> I've everything that anybody could ever hope for, but one thing—a sense of closeness to my children and wife. While I made my fortune, my children grew up strangers to me, and my wife found her fulfillment outside of our relationship. Now, nothing has much value.

The problem? Traveling too heavy—too many weights—too many sins.

Step Three: Set a Secure Course!

. . . *looking unto Jesus* . . . The real intent of Hebrews 12:2 is to bring into clear focus the full image of Christ in our lives and to chart a course that will navigate the rough seas and rocky shores under His guidance.

The writer of Hebrews knew that we confront a brainwashed world, a pressure-cooker world that stretches us to the breaking point. He knew that we could lose our sense of objectivity, our sense of absolutes, our sense of divine identity, and our sense of spiritual values.

The brain is the most complex mechanism ever created. In one way it is like a telephone switchboard that connects incoming and outgoing calls. In another way it is like a computer that makes decisions about which circuits to link and which calls to connect. However, the crowning achievement of the brain is the capacity to think, perceive, and experience. Further, the way in which these three processes combine determines what we call learning. In turn, what we learn and how we evaluate this new information shape our behavior and chart the course we pursue.

The essential element is to program our brains with the power of Christ so that we can truly fix our minds on "whatsoever things are true . . . just . . . pure . . . lovely . . . of good report" (Phil. 4:8).

Step Four: Hang Tough!

. . . endure chastening . . . strengthen the hands which hang down, and the feeble knees . . . make straight paths for your feet, so that what is lame may not be dislocated, but rather be healed (Heb. 12:7,12,13). The procedure for hanging tough is trusting the Lord to help us convert bad stress to good. Susan Seliger gives a definitive overview of this process of converting bad stress to good:

> Bad stress can inflict real bodily harm. First it can lower resistance to disease. . . . If bad stress is occasional, the body's immune system can bounce back. If it is prolonged, the immune system is thrown out of whack. Second, repeated and unremitting episodes of bad stress mean repeated release of adrenaline. If the problem prompts no physical exertion to use up the adrenaline—and most stresses in modern life are of a mental rather than a physical nature—then excess adrenaline will remain in your system and can play a part in the buildup of cholesterol in your arteries that can lead to heart disease.
>
> The most important key to defusing distress is to become conscious of that inner voice you have. Perhaps you are constantly assessing yourself and your environment and reporting silently to yourself: "This looks threatening; I don't think I can handle it."

Many people are not conscious of this internal commentator, but if you learn to listen to the way you talk to yourself, you may find that you are usually not being as encouraging as you could be—that you are actually making matters worse for yourself.

Instead of standing in the line at the bank, checking your watch and listening to your inner voice computing how late you will be to your appointment and wondering why you didn't get cash for the weekend yesterday, you should make your inner voice be soothing: "I don't like waiting in this line, but there is nothing I can do about it now, so I might as well relax. Look how tense everyone else is getting. It's actually kind of funny."

Another trick is to stop thinking about the time. It may be slipping by, but counting the seconds only fritters away energy and activates the stress response. Time consciousness, or "hurry sickness," is a key personality trait of the heart-attack-prone personality. One stress researcher says she found that simply removing her wristwatch for several weeks greatly reduced the time pressures she felt.

To convert bad stress to good, remember the following:

Before an event expected to be stressful, visualize what may take place. Such a rehearsal will make the actual event seem familiar, helping you to relax and handle the situation with confidence.

During a tense situation, such as taking a test or meeting a tight deadline, talk nicely to yourself; don't harp on poor preparation or performance. Instead, you should make your inner voice offer praise and reassurance.

Afterward, luxuriate in the relief of the burden's being lifted. Even if things didn't go so well, avoid puritanical self-criticism. This refreshing interlude can help strengthen your system to better resist the wear and tear of future distress.

"Any bad stress can be turned around," insists Dr. [Kenneth] Greenspan, "if you take steps that make you feel that you are controlling your life and it isn't controlling you."[2]

Take a minute and consider the following seven telltale signs of bad stress as taken from the article "Stress Can Be Good For You":

1. Cold hands, especially if one is colder than the other.
2. Indigestion, diarrhea, too-frequent urination.
3. Being susceptible to every cold or virus that goes around (which could mean that the physical strains of distress are weakening your immune system).
4. Muscle spasms or a soreness and tightness in the jaw, back of the neck, shoulders or lower back.
5. Shortness of breath.
6. Headaches, tiredness, sleeping too much or too little.
7. Becoming suddenly accident prone.[3]

When we recognize any of these signals, we should stop what we are doing—if only for two or three minutes—take several deep breaths and try to relax. In this state of relaxation it is then important for us to focus our faith on the person and work of Jesus Christ as we appropriate by His Spirit the power to handle pressure. With our faith in focus, we can be filled with joy and face whatever our circumstances bring us.

9 *Stress Point*

The Peril of Negative Circumstances

NEUTRALIZING YOUR NEGATIVES

Scriptural Source

2 Corinthians 6:1–10

Joy Sustainers

Translate the transformed life
Personalize the productive laws
Maintain an optimistic outlook
Live by a code of commendation

9

NEUTRALIZING YOUR NEGATIVES

Whether we like it or not, negatives are a part of life. We are struck by tragedy, and we have to deal with grief. We are taken advantage of, and we have to deal with anger. We are ripped off, and we have to deal with rage. We are abandoned (either physically or emotionally), and we have to deal with bitterness. We lose everything, and we have to deal with failure. We come in second, and we have to deal with defeat. We experience repeated setbacks, and we have to deal with a poor self-image.

The problem is not so much encountering the negatives but finding a way to neutralize them so that we don't lose our joy and life doesn't become a terrible drag. In fact, one of the precipitating factors in suicide is a feeling that there are no more alternatives, that all the exits have been closed.

There is good news, however, in the message of the Bible because it was given to us by inspiration of the Holy Spirit. The Bible speaks to us at our lowest and raises us to our highest. Scripture finds us at our weakest points and transforms us into our strongest selves. Within its truths an eternal dimension picks us up at our saddest and rejuvenates us to experience the highest joy.

TRANSLATE THE TRANSFORMED LIFE

In effect the Bible gives us the power to neutralize the negatives by giving us the power to be transformed. To maintain joy is to live the transformed life. To be transformed is to change form completely, as illustrated in the transfiguration of Christ (see Matt. 17) or the transition of a caterpillar into a butterfly. To be transformed is to undergo a spiritual metamorphosis, to live in a state of renewal. A transformed life produces a character molded progressively toward the excellency of Christ.

If we feel in control of our lives, we can channel the negative stresses that come from conflict and pressure into positive forces that make us healthier and stronger than those persons who avoid conflict and competition altogether. Further, the most recent research points out that the ability to control stress from negatives is within our own power.[1] The attitude we have about ourselves and our environment most influences whether we will be hurt by the negatives or neutralize them by transformed living.

PERSONALIZE THE PRODUCTIVE LAWS

We live the transformed life by using the laws that produce the positives and neutralize the negatives. We cannot escape the pressures and problems of life; rather, we assert our spiritual authority over them by governing our behavior by the New Testament concepts of productive living.

Too often we get pushed around by Murphy's Law—If anything can go wrong, it will. Then we get caught in O'Toole's Commentary on Murphy's Law—Murphy was an optimist. To make matters worse, we seem to shortchange ourselves with Jennings's Corollary—The chance of the bread falling with the buttered side down is directly proportional to the cost of the carpet. The final result is Bowen's First Law—When in doubt, mumble!

Joy, however, comes as we cope with the negative forces of living through the productive application of the laws of God's Word.

For instance, think about the spiritual law of *cause and effect.* Luke 6:38 says, "Give, and it will be given to you: good measure, pressed down, shaken together, and running over, will be put into your bosom. For with the same measure that you use, it will be measured back to you."

A reciprocal happening takes place in this law of Christ. When we give productively, we receive bountifully, and the result is that we live joyously.

This is best illustrated by the testimony of a man who lost his business, suffered through a divorce, and ended up on skid row. A street ministry reached him, and he began the long journey back to productivity and solvency. He found a job—but he needed a hundred and fifty dollars to make a deposit on an apartment. With only twenty dollars in his pocket, he wandered the streets, not sure what to do. He chanced to meet a street derelict who "hit him up" for a meal. Identifying with him, the man compassionately gave the derelict the twenty dollars—and he found himself not only with no place to live but also broke. Ducking into an alley, he prayed earnestly for God's direction. He then decided to spend the night at the mission, and it was there that a ministry team from our church recognized him. One of the team members—inspired by the Holy Spirit—gave him two hundred dollars! The man had given *productively* and had received *bountifully*.

Next, think about the spiritual law of *ask and receive.* Matthew 7:7,8 states, "Ask, and it will be given to you; seek, and you will find; knock, and it will be opened to you. For everyone who asks receives, and he who seeks finds, and to him who knocks, it will be opened." There is a productive relationship here. God responds as we come boldly to His throne in the same way that a loving earthly father responds to a child—whatever decisions are made will be effected for the highest good. Christ, Himself, told us, "If you, then, being evil, know how to give good gifts to your children, how much more will your Father who is in heaven give good things to those who ask Him!" (Matt. 7:11).

Then, think about the spiritual law of *relate and agree*. Matthew 18:19 gives us the truth that if any two believers on earth agree about anything they ask for, it will be done by the Father in heaven. Verse 20 tells us, "For where two or three are gathered together in My name, I am there in the midst of them."

The neutralizing effect comes into play through the joining of common faith and belief in claiming the heritage we have in Christ. His message to us is, "Whatever you bind on earth will be bound in heaven, and whatever you loose on earth will be loosed in heaven" (Matt. 18:18). When two or more people come together in like mind and heart under the lordship of Jesus Christ and agree on the principles revealed in the Word, the power of confirming the covenant promises is released so that negatives are neutralized and positives are set free.

As John 14:12 puts it, "I say to you, he who believes in Me, the works that I do he will do also; and greater works than these he will do, because I go to My Father."

The Kelly family put these laws into effect when every visible sign said there was absolutely no hope financially or emotionally. The family business went bankrupt. All of their valuable personal belongings and assets were taken by the court. Their beautiful home was lost. The two oldest children had to drop out of college. The wife was diagnosed with multiple sclerosis, and the husband suffered a mild heart attack—all in the space of one year.

What do we do when we have to look up to see bottom? We activate the spiritual laws and trust God with the details.

The Kellys had a family conference and decided to pull together as one unit. After the two college girls dropped out of school, they went to work. The father started a new business from scratch. The mother took the multiple sclerosis in stride and through prayer and the wonders of medical science watched it go into remission.

Every night as a family they repeated these spiritual laws in prayer and mutual reinforcement. They pooled their resources, and soon the family business was flourishing again. Now, five years later, the girls are finishing college. The father has posted a business comeback, and the mother's condition remains stable.

THE CORINTHIAN CASE

Perhaps the most appropriate illustration of these principles is found in Paul's letters to the Corinthians.

As outlined in the first letter, the Corinthian church was plagued with negatives. There was doctrinal error about baptism and the meaning of the Resurrection. The people had become carnal and worldly in their habits. They defiled their bodies and tolerated extreme immorality.

In addition, confusion about marriage and interpersonal conflicts were widespread. Fellow believers were suing each other in court.

To make matters worse, the worship experience had deteriorated. There was gross abuse of the purpose and practice of the Lord's Supper, together with wholesale corruption of the exercise of the gifts of the Spirit.

Put all of this together, and it spells negatives with a capital *N*.

The apostle Paul, however, was undaunted in the face of what appeared to be mass chaos. Rather than be defeated and lose the positive effects of the gospel message, Paul wrote a second letter to the Corinthians and made a powerful case for the positive insights of the gospel. From his personal experience under the anointing of the Holy Spirit, Paul described the good news of the Word of Christ as being (1) *triumphant:* Christ has power over our problems (see 2 Cor. 2:14–16); (2) *sincere:* We can trust its power and presence (see 2 Cor. 2:17); (3) *approved:* We are His letters read and known of all men (see 2 Cor. 3:1,2); (4) *authentic:* We set forth the truth (see 2 Cor. 4:2); (5) *confident:* We have a building from God, an eternal house in heaven, not built by human hands (see 2 Cor. 5:1–9); and (6) *committed:* As servants of God we commend ourselves in every way (see 2 Cor. 6:1–8).

This Corinthian case is a classic example of neutralizing negatives through the power of the gospel of Jesus Christ. Further, in a practical way Paul shared a twofold plan for really making it happen.

MAINTAIN AN OPTIMISTIC OUTLOOK

We then, as fellow workers together with Him also plead with you
not to receive the grace of God in vain. For He says:
"In an acceptable time I have heard you,
And in the day of salvation I have helped you."
Behold, now is the accepted time; behold, now is the day
of salvation. We give no offense in anything, that our ministry
may not be blamed (2 Cor. 6:1–3).

Optimism is "the inclination to put the most favorable construction on all actions and events." Optimism anticipates the best possible outcomes of every happening, regardless of how negative.

Thus, Paul told the Corinthians and the message is relayed to us that we did not receive God's grace in vain. Rather, we can anticipate the power of salvation when we need it. As an example, we are not to put a stumbling block in anyone's way with negative expressions. Instead, "in all things we commend ourselves as ministers of God" (2 Cor. 6:4).

Paul didn't respond to the Corinthian problem with apathy, overreaction, fear, anger, bitterness, or any of the other negative emotions that rob us of joy. In the face of it all, he maintained an optimistic attitude that neutralized the negatives.

I experienced this neutralizing effect of optimism while visiting with a family that was forced to move from a million-dollar mansion into a cramped apartment because of severe business reversals during the recession of the early seventies.

This entrepreneur struck it big during the boom times, extended himself too far, took it on the chin, and lost everything when the recession hit.

On moving day I arrived to offer condolences and support. The house was stripped bare, and what few things remained had been loaded on a truck.

Upon arriving, I was surprised to be greeted by a cheery housewife who said, "Pastor Walker! Glad to see you! You're just in time to share with us in our last devotion in this house. Isn't it wonderful? God helped us save the organ, and we are going to have our family devotion around that organ before we put it in the truck."

Amazed at such a positive attitude, I wondered what they would sing. It seemed appropriate to me to do a few bars of "Nobody Knows The Trouble I See," or perhaps it would be more fitting to do the funeral dirge "Saul"! After all, what could be worse than losing everything you worked for?

To my surprise, however, we all gathered around the organ— husband, four kids, wife at the keyboard, and me, the pastor.

Without a tear or a vocal tremble, the entire family broke out in the doxology:

> Praise God, from whom all blessings flow,
> Praise Him, all creatures here below,
> Praise Him above, ye heavenly host,
> Praise Father, Son, and Holy Ghost.

I was ministered to more than I ministered. It has been over ten years now, and I have watched that family's material resources slowly build back until, in the husband's words, "God gave it all back to us, but now we are much better stewards of all His many blessings."

LIVE BY A CODE OF COMMENDATION

But in all things we commend ourselves as ministers of God: in much patience, in tribulations, in needs, in distresses, in stripes, in imprisonments, in tumults, in labors, in sleeplessness, in fastings; by purity, by knowledge, by longsuffering, by kindness, by the Holy Spirit, by sincere love, by the word of truth, by the power of God, by the armor of righteousness on the right hand and on the left, by honor and dishonor, by evil report and good report; as deceivers, and yet true; as unknown, and yet well known; as dying, and behold we live; as chastened, and yet not killed; as sorrowful, yet always rejoicing; as poor, yet making many rich; as having nothing, and yet possessing all things (2 Cor. 6:4–10).

Every person has a code of ethics. Even individuals who say they have no code actually live by a no-code code.

The apostle Paul declared that we are to commend ourselves

in all things. As it is used here, *to commend* means "to show, demonstrate, approve, or manifest." He also said we are to live as ministers of God, that is, as persons whose deepest desire is to do the will of the Lord. Thus, we are to demonstrate our willingness to serve God in every circumstance.

Finally, Paul set up a series of possible situations and called for a *code of commendation* that demonstrates to the world we are true ministers of Jesus Christ.

As I reflected on this notion, it suddenly dawned on me one day that I needed my own code of commendation to see me through the tough times. In this process of meditation, seven concepts came to mind triggered by seven basic words. These are as follows:

1. *Constancy.* Conditions are always changing; therefore, I must not be dependent on temporary happenings.

2. *Consecration.* The most important element in my life is my relationship with Jesus Christ, and this relationship must continually be enhanced through a deepened release and sacrifice of my selfhood to Christ.

3. *Commitment.* God is concerned about me as my Father, and nothing happens to me apart from my dedication to Him.

4. *Contentment.* Whatever happens in my life is under the providential working of God in my life; thus, I must accept the fact that God's will and ways are beyond my full comprehension.

5. *Consistency.* Every situation in my life is significantly influenced by God's love; thus, my mission in life is to experience God's loving-kindness regardless of the circumstantial evidence.

6. *Correlation.* My world- and life-views must see circumstances and situations not as ends in themselves but as parts of God's kingdom at work in me.

7. *Consummation.* I must see my present circumstances and situations as only temporary and preparatory experiences for my real life in the joy and glory of eternity with God.

In these seven statements I have found new insight into neutralizing negatives and living in the positives reflected in the Word.

Perhaps these concepts sound too theoretical to some people who will wonder if they really work. In response I offer this letter:

> Three years ago when I was 26 years old, I learned what it means to have joy in the midst of trials. At that time I was a successful systems analyst, had a wonderful marriage, and became a father for the first time in June of that year. That summer in response to prayer and God's guidance, I quit my job; we moved to a new town, and I entered seminary full-time to prepare myself for the ministry.
>
> This was a stressful time for me because, in addition to having to adjust to a new baby, my self-esteem took a beating due to the lack of income and status together with the difficulties of my studies.
>
> Finally in November, two weeks before my first set of final exams, my wife became ill and died. Suddenly, I was a widower with a five-month-old daughter, over five hundred miles from the nearest relative. It seemed that my world had collapsed.
>
> Yet I didn't despair because I knew that the Lord was real, that He loves me, that He is in control of events even though they are not pleasant and I don't understand them.
>
> The verses that I held on to and believe that became real to me were Romans 8:28, Isaiah 41:10, and Philippians 4:13.
>
> In my experience the strength and joy of God were activated by faith and belief in His complete goodness; by praise in the face of heartbreak; by the prayers of myself and many others on my behalf; by the body of believers coming to my aid in so many ways, I found that the Lord is able to sustain us through anything if we turn to Him.

We can't escape it! We live in a negative world, but the challenge is to keep our joy by maintaining an optimistic outlook and living by a personalized code of commendation.

10 *Stress Point*

The Trauma of Tragic Experiences

TRANSCENDING YOUR TRAGEDIES

Scriptural
Sources

Philippians 1:6
Romans 8:26–31
Romans 8:35–39

Joy
Sustainers

Know God works for good
Know God finishes what He starts
Know the Holy Spirit makes intercession
Know God keeps us in His love

10

TRANSCENDING YOUR TRAGEDIES

Thanksgiving Day 1980 was family day at Grandmother's house in Tennessee. It was a day of laughter, songs, play, and general fellowship with uncles, aunts, cousins, and extended families all coming together to form one great nuclear family. It was one of those perfect days of family interaction and reunion.

Little did we know that just thirty-six hours later a tragic phone call would come informing us that our son, Paul Dana, and his wife, Julie, had been involved in a head-on automobile collision on the way home from the celebration.

Early in the morning in a motel room in Tennessee, I picked up the phone and heard an unknown voice from a faceless doctor say, "Your son and his wife have had an accident. Julie is seriously injured, but she will recover. Your son was killed instantly. Where do you want us to send his body?" Only those who have experienced this shock can understand the dull ache and fearful dread that are experienced in such a tragedy. In a terrible moment the joyous closeness of Thanksgiving changed to the empty loss of death. The joy of a firstborn son who fulfilled every expectation and brought nothing but pleasure and pride was changed to numbness. *This can't possibly be true! Somebody tell us that this is all a big mistake!*

What do we do when tragedy strikes? We hurt. We hurt when

we have to confront the tragedy of divorce. We hurt when we have to face the tragedy that our children have become drug addicts. We hurt when we deal with the tragedy of bankruptcy. We hurt when we get the tragic news that the tumor is malignant and the prognosis is not good. We hurt when we experience the finality of a loved one's death.

But we also do something else—we turn to the deepest resources within us and draw upon the rudiments of our faith to sustain us.

THE MESSAGE

The sustenance by faith is the message God gave to Job. The Bible says that Job was a perfect man—a righteous man—a man who turned from evil. Nonetheless, in one fell swoop everything that had meaning and purpose or made sense for Job was lost. The Sabeans rustled all his oxen and donkeys and killed all the herdsmen. Fire struck the sheep and the shepherds and burned them up. The Chaldeans raided the camels, carried them off, and put all the drivers to death. A whirlwind swept across the desert, struck his eldest son's house, and killed all of Job's sons and daughters while they were dining (see Job 1:13–19).

To top it off, Job broke out in running sores from head to foot, and in disgust his wife said to him, "Do you still hold fast to your integrity? Curse God and die!" (Job 2:9).

There he was. Job the righteous. Job the affluent. Job the successful. Job the powerful. Everything was gone. Everything was wiped out.

What did Job do? He was a sick man sitting in an ash pile. What did he do when the bottom dropped out?

Notice his action: "Then Job arose, tore his robe, and shaved his head; and he fell to the ground and worshiped" (Job 1:20).

Rather strange, isn't it? Everything was lost, and Job fell down on the ground and worshiped.

Notice his attitude: "In all this Job did not sin nor charge God with wrong" (Job 1:22). Notice how he expressed his faith: "For I know that my Redeemer lives, / And He shall stand at last on the earth; / And after my skin is destroyed, this I know, / That in my flesh I shall see God" (Job 19:25,26).

What a fantastic outlook! Job learned the essential message— *we can transcend our tragedies!*

A similar kind of testimony came from the apostle Paul.

Look at all he had to undergo: "perils . . . weariness and toil . . . sleeplessness . . . hunger and thirst . . . fastings . . . cold and nakedness" (2 Cor. 11:26,27).

Look at all he had to suffer: that inexplicable thorn in the flesh. The J. B. Phillips translation calls it "a physical handicap—one of Satan's angels—to harass [him] and effectually stop any conceit" (2 Cor. 12:7).

How did Paul handle it? In his words,

> Concerning this thing I pleaded with the Lord three times that it might depart from me. And He said to me, "My grace is sufficient for you, for My strength is made perfect in weakness." Therefore most gladly I will rather boast in my infirmities, that the power of Christ may rest upon me (2 Cor. 12:8,9).

Paul found a resource in the sufficient grace of God that enabled him to live by the Spirit regardless of what occurred in his life. For him, grace meant contentment regardless of the circumstances, contentment regardless of the situation. His was a contentment that transcended tragedy (see Phil. 4:11–13).

However, the beautiful thing about this transcendent life is that it is still available for us today. We can transcend tragedy in our own experiences, in our own traumas.

Mel was talking about this in the following letter. He learned how to transcend the tragedy of meaninglessness and despair through the message of God's grace.

Most of my thirty-eight years on this earth has been a struggle one way or the other. Life has been one big, continuous hassle. I grew up in a difficult home environment. My first "adult" experience in life involved man's inhumanity to man in Southeast Asia. After returning to civilian life I realized that a form of that inhumanity seemed to be a pervasive part of our own society. By the age of twenty-one I was bitter and cynical about life in general. I turned to drugs and alcohol for solace. I became chronically depressed. I attempted suicide. Neither psychotherapy or legal psychotherapeutic drugs had any lasting affect. Ultimately I lost everything I valued both materially and emotionally. My wife and two sons were all that I had left that I cared for, and I lost them.

I have been living alone most of the last four years. I made a decision last year that I was going to find a purpose for my existence and being or I was going to commit suicide and do it successfully this time. I had tried everything else in life in the pursuit of happiness. The only thing left was to try Jesus Christ, and nothing has been the same since.

Life now has a new sense of purpose and meaning. For the first time in my life I feel a happiness and peace that defies human expression or exclamation.

I don't want to misconstrue that my life has become instant "peaches and cream." It hasn't! I still have some tough emotional issues to deal with along with life's everyday problems. What is different now is that I don't have to tackle the problems by myself. The presence of the Holy Spirit within me is real and very strong. I have turned my life over to Him for guidance and control. What a difference it has made! I have discovered the value of prayer for they are really being answered.

There aren't any human words that appropriately express my thanks to God for revealing Himself to me . . .

This is the essential message: "I don't have to tackle the problems myself. The presence of the Holy Spirit within me is real and very strong. I have turned my life over to Him for guidance and control. What a difference it has made!"

THE MEANING

The meaning of faith is *to become a transcender:* to go beyond the limits, to step over the boundaries, to surpass the limiting factors, to rise above the hindrances, to cope with the uncontrollable.

But how are we to accomplish this? Sometimes it seems so futile.

Perhaps we can identify with the classic story of the people on an international flight. After flying about two hours over the Atlantic Ocean, the pilot spoke to the passengers via the intercom and said, "Ladies and gentlemen, I regret to inform you that the number one engine has just gone out, but don't be alarmed. We can make it fine on three engines."

A few minutes later the pilot spoke again and said, "Ladies and gentlemen, I regret to inform you that the number two engine just went out, but don't be alarmed. We can make it fine on two engines."

A few minutes later the pilot spoke a third time and said, "Ladies and gentlemen, I regret to inform you that the number three engine just stopped. If you will all move to the right of the plane and look down at the ocean, you will see a little dot. That dot is a life raft, and on that life raft are your pilot and crew. This is a recording."

Sometimes we feel that same sense of futility, particularly when we are confronted with a tragedy over which we have no control.

Regardless of our position in Christ or our place in life, there are those times when "the nations raged, the kingdoms were moved" (Ps. 46:6). It is in these moments that we recognize the importance of hammering out a transcendent faith even in the midst of extreme frustration. In this regard the apostle Paul said, "We are hard pressed on every side, but not crushed; we are perplexed, but not in despair; persecuted, but not forsaken; struck down, but not destroyed—always carrying about in the body the dying of the Lord Jesus, that the life of Jesus also may be manifested in our body" (2 Cor. 4:8–10).

In other words we carry the death of Jesus in order to make the life of Jesus a truly viable force. However, when we read these verses, we come face-to-face with the question, Why are these crises in our lives? No answer is quite adequate, and we may have to be content with Christ's words, "I still have many things to say to you, but you cannot bear them now" (John 16:12). The truth is that both Christians and non-Christians make up the *statistical probabilities of life*. Christians die of heart attacks, cancer, accidents, war, and all of the other hazards that make up our broken world. We are in a limited situation because of the fallout of the Fall. We are all subject to the randomization and unpredictability of a world under the domination of the prince of the power of the air (see Eph. 2:2).

THE MAINTENANCE

Nonetheless, in the midst of these negatives, the Bible makes it very clear that God has given us "exceedingly great and precious promises, that through these [we] may be partakers of the divine nature, having escaped the corruption that is in the world through lust" (2 Pet. 1:4).

In this same regard, Paul told us that

the Spirit Himself bears witness with our spirit that we are children of God, and if children, then heirs—heirs of God and joint heirs with Christ, if indeed we suffer with Him, that we may also be glorified together. . . . we also who have the firstfruits of the Spirit, even we ourselves groan within ourselves, eagerly waiting for the adoption, the redemption of our body (Rom. 8:16,17,23).

Thus, we hear the psalmist say, "The LORD of hosts is with us; / The God of Jacob is our refuge" (Ps. 46:7). But what are these precious promises? How may we be heirs of God and joint heirs with Christ? What can we expect if the God of Jacob is our refuge? How do we maintain equilibrium?

First, *we can expect God to work for good in all things*. This is the universal promise of Romans 8:28. Although everything that happens to us is not necessarily within itself good—it often hurts—we know that the long-term effects of every situation blend together for a symphony of eternal good under the direction of the Father.

Second, *we can expect God to finish what He has begun in our lives*. This is the promise of Philippians 1:6, "being confident of this very thing, that He who has begun a good work in you will complete it until the day of Jesus Christ." One translator says, "You will see that it is finished" (PHILLIPS). It doesn't really matter how small or how large our faith may be. God will nourish our faith until it grows to the size He desires. In God's mind the plan formulated is just as good as the plan accomplished. We will some day be glorified because God completes every work that He begins (see Phil. 3:21).

Third, *we can expect the Spirit to make intercession when we are having problems*. Paul exclaimed in Romans 8:31, "If God is for us, who can be against us?" God affirms, and He also acts on our behalf. He actually promises to give us victory in the midst of crisis. Paul declared in Romans 8:37, "Yet in all these things we are more than conquerors through Him who loved us." Inside ourselves we have the capacity to overcome, even though we have to be resigned to the fallout of a frustrated creation, the limitations of human weakness and the continuing problem of evil promoted by a secularized world view. In this regard Peg Rankin states:

> We know that to take a job after a period of unemployment is to conquer even if the job lasts only temporarily. To become resigned to the death of a spouse is to conquer, even though we may still have to overcome moments of overwhelming depression. To receive physical healing is to conquer, even though we know that we will get sick again and eventually die. But what does it mean to be "*more* than a conqueror"? Perhaps it means to go on with Christ in glory where conditions are permanent, not temporary. Perhaps that is why "the others" in Hebrews 11 did not accept deliverance. They were looking for "a better resurrection."[1]

The transcendent life is an interceding life as we depend upon the Spirit to fulfill the meaning of Romans 8:27, "Now He who searches the hearts knows what the mind of the Spirit is, because He makes intercession for the saints according to the will of God."

Fourth, *we can expect God to keep us in His love.* The Scriptures say,

> Who shall separate us from the love of Christ? Shall tribulation, or distress, or persecution, or famine, or nakedness, or peril, or sword? . . . I am persuaded that neither death nor life, nor angels nor principalities nor powers, nor things present nor things to come, nor height nor depth nor any other created thing, shall be able to separate us from the love of God which is in Christ Jesus our Lord (Rom. 8:35–39).

This everlasting love of God was vividly illustrated in the life of the Hoffman family. In the space of a year one daugher divorced, a second daughter was imprisoned, and the father died.

In spite of the pain and even in the midst of this intense suffering, the transcendent life emerged.

These are the words of the mother:

> When *pain* comes, it comes in piercing, specific jolts. That's what I felt when we received a phone call that Barbara had been arrested. The pain seemed to stay in the very pit of my stomach and never left for months. It seemed to just hit in different degrees with each event that took place after her arrest. I thought then this is the worst thing that could ever happen. I began to wonder where God was in this intense pain that wouldn't stop hurting. I spent so much time trying to figure out why we were all having to go through this before I decided how I would respond to this tragedy. I had a choice to either give up or face this head on and trust God that He would see us through. I am glad I chose to trust my Heavenly Father because He has been faithful . . .
>
> When the doctor sat across from my husband and me and told us he had Hodgkin's disease, the same intense pain hit me again. I thought this is it, this was more than I could bear.
>
> I was so afraid! Fear had taken over. How could I make it without Gary? How could I handle Barbara's situation? And Michael is only 11 years old; he needs a father. So for a year and a half I watched Gary dwindle away and each day the Lord gave me strength to take care of him and prepare me for the days ahead without him. God used all this pain in its grossest form to teach me to turn to Him and totally trust Him.
>
> Knowing He has hurt with me and cried with me and loved me through His Spirit, and through members of His body who have lifted me up, I can face tomorrow.

Here are the words of the incarcerated daughter who, during the first two years of her imprisonment, has completed a year of college and has lived an exemplary Christian life as a witness to the entire prison:

151

I know I did wrong, but I have confessed my sins and know I am forgiven . . .

I know that God is my only hope, and I'll never lose my faith. I know the Lord hears our prayers, and soon they will be answered.

Here are the words of the father in a letter to the personnel of his company written just before his death:

I wanted to write this letter to all my friends and co-workers to let each of you know that life, or anything you believe in, is worth fighting for. I am writing to encourage you not to give up in any area of your life or in the life of this beloved company.

Perhaps it is because of recent events that I feel I must write this letter. As most of you know our daughter is now serving a prison sentence.

In the same year I started itching, and at first the doctor attributed my itch to stress and anxiety. But then I developed a high fever. The doctor discovered that my lymph nodes were enlarged, and a biopsy confirmed the diagnosis of Hodgkin's disease.

Giving up would probably have been a more logical route and certainly easier at times than hanging in there and fighting. That's when I began to praise God that He had given me a fighting spirit. He knew that I was going to need one.

From the beginning of our tragedy with our daughter and through this past year, you have never left our side. I am proud and grateful to be a part of a company like you. You have shown me and my family love and compassion through your concern and prayers. Someone once said, "Pity weeps and runs away . . . compassion comes to help and stay." Thank you for helping and staying.

People who never, never, never give up eventually become winners. Isn't it time that all of us forget about how bad things are and begin to dwell on the good, the positive. In the words of Saint Paul, "Forgetting the past and looking forward to what lies ahead, I strain to reach the end of the race and receive the prize for which God is calling us up to heaven because of what Christ Jesus did for us" (Phil. 3:13,14 TLB).

God bless each of you.

The transcendent approach makes us understand that whole, unbruised, unbroken persons are of little use to God. The only way we can learn *agape* love is through the circumstances of life that mold us into the pliability that allows love to operate. Agape love is the giving of self without regard for receiving in return. This law of love is the supreme law of eternity. The problem is that this love has to be learned within the confines of time. Only upon this earth and in this environment can this transcendent triumph of God's love be molded in such a way that we will be qualified to administer the law of love in eternity. Billheimer makes the point that natural affection does not have to be learned. Agape love is only learned by being utterly broken, by suffering without resentment.[2]

Once we learn this lesson of the transcendent life, the very meaning of 2 Corinthians 1:3-5 comes alive in a new and literal way:

> Blessed be the God and Father of our Lord Jesus Christ, the Father of mercies and God of all comfort, who comforts us in all our tribulation, that we may be able to comfort those who are in any trouble, with the comfort with which we ourselves are comforted by God.

We are not immune from tragedy. The good news, however, is that we can keep our joy by learning to live the life of transcendence. We can be sustained by the fact that "the LORD of hosts is with us; / The God of Jacob is our refuge" (Ps. 46:11).

11 *Stress Point*

The Difficulty of Time Management

TREASURING YOUR TIME

Scriptural Source   Ecclesiastes 3:1–14

Joy Sustainers

Analyze
Synchronize
Spiritualize
Programize
Personalize

11

TREASURING YOUR TIME

There is an old saying, Time waits for no one. As old as it is and as many times as it has been used, this saying still conveys a relevant message—that time management and happiness go hand in hand. Or to put it another way, the way we use our time is a barometer for the level of our joy. We are what we do, and doing obviously involves the utilization of time.

By its very nature, time makes us or breaks us. We get pressured because we run out of time. We erode relationships because we are indifferent with our time. We lose money because of our poor use of time. We make needless errors because of the inadequate organization of our time.

The writer of Ecclesiastes—The Teacher—told us that "to everything there is a season, / A time for every purpose under heaven" (Eccles. 3:1). This passage reminds us of the importance of treasuring our time, because the joy of life is directly correlated to the investment of our time.

In this regard I recently ran a check on several married couples I had counseled during the past two years. These couples were chosen at random, and to my surprise, scheduling and the use of time were very prominent in causing conflict in the majority of the cases.

Thus, when we talk about treasuring our time, we are not simply mouthing theoretical nonsense. Time is a precious gift from God, and its use is a determining factor in whether we live a life of joy or succumb to the hectic struggle.

THE CONCERN

Because time is a precious gift, the biblical message is concerned with the *brevity of time*. Psalm 90:12 petitions God by saying, "So teach us to number our days, / That we may gain a heart of wisdom." Ecclesiastes 12:1 gives the admonition to "remember now your Creator in the days of your youth, / Before the difficult days come, / And the years draw near when you say, / 'I have no pleasure in them.' " First Corinthians 7:29 warns that "the time is short," and verse 31 says that "the form of this world is passing away."

The apostle Paul was concerned about the *utilization of time* in the most productive way, and he cautioned the Ephesians to be careful how they live, "not as fools but as wise, redeeming the time, because the days are evil" (Eph. 5:15). He expressed the same urgency to the Colossians and told them to be wise in the way they act toward outsiders "redeeming the time" (Col. 4:5).

If we want balance, productivity, order, tranquillity, congruence, peace, and joy in our lives, it is important for us to share this biblical concern so that we, too, redeem the time. We need to make the most of every opportunity.

THE CONTROL

The secret for treasuring our time is control, not only in setting our schedules but in disciplining ourselves to keep our commitments. We can't manufacture, market, or store time, but we can learn the meaning of control. In fact, this is what The Teacher had in mind when he said that God has made everything beautiful in its time (see Eccles. 3:11).

He then went on to explain the meaning of this statement by saying, "Also He has put eternity in their hearts, except that no one can find out the work that God does from beginning to end" (Eccles. 3:11).

Having established the importance of time, The Teacher moved ahead with a personal note and shared, "I know that nothing is better for them than to rejoice, and to do good in their lives, and also that every man should eat and drink and enjoy the good of all his labor—it is the gift of God" (Eccles. 3:12,13).

Here is our challenge: We are to use time in such a way that we can rejoice and do good, because we all want to eat, drink, and find enjoyment in our life's work.

The consideration, however, is for us to recognize what The Teacher told us in verse 14, "I know that whatever God does, / It shall be forever. / Nothing can be added to it, / And nothing taken from it. / God does it, that men should fear before Him." The control of our time has at its base the reverence of God and respect for the gift of life.

THE CONTEXT

With this scriptural basis for treasuring our time before us, it is necessary to live our lives in the context of God's will for the use of our time. Like the writer of Ecclesiastes, we sense the ambivalence of life and share his concern that materialism leads to a mind-set that cries out, "Vanity of vanities . . . / All is vanity" (Eccles. 12:8).

We recognize that we have a duty to God and are held responsible for the use of the resources He gives us. Thus, we agree with

The Teacher, "Let us hear the conclusion of the whole matter: / Fear God and keep His commandments, / For this is man's all" (Eccles. 12:13).

The point is that we need to have a *biblical philosophy of time* that frees us from the tyranny of the world's rat race as we arrange our priorities with God first, others second, and ourselves last. Without a biblical philosophy of time we find ourselves saying, "I really want to increase my prayer life, but I just don't have time." "I would really like to improve the relationship with my spouse and family, but I just don't have time." "I honestly want to become more involved in the work of the church and its ministries, but I just don't have time." "I wish I could do more personal things and really grow as a person and a Christian, but I just don't have time." "I really need to exercise, but I just don't have time."

So, what is a biblical philosophy of time?

EVERY GOOD GIFT COMES FROM GOD

In our modern age we have learned to do many things. We have split the atom, harnessed computers, and ushered in the space age, but the genius behind it all is a gift from God. As The Teacher said, "He has put eternity in their hearts" (Eccles. 3:11). In other words, we are to live our lives in such a way that we see every good gift as a blessing from God.

Moses had to constantly remind Israel of this, and in Deuteronomy 8:18 we hear him say, "And you shall remember the LORD your God, for it is He who gives you power to get wealth, that He may establish His covenant which He swore to your fathers, as it is this day."

Time and time again the prophets reminded Israel of the same theme, and Haggai echoed the words of the Lord, " 'The silver is Mine, and the gold is Mine,' says the LORD of hosts" (Hag. 2:8).

In the New Testament, James unequivocally stated, "Every good gift and every perfect gift is from above, and comes down from the Father of lights, with whom there is no variation or shadow of turning" (James 1:17).

Our problem is we get caught in the Nebuchadnezzar syndrome. We forget the source of our blessings.

In Daniel 4, Nebuchadnezzar, the king of Babylon, walked on his balcony and overlooked the greatest city in the world during that era. There he was, the man who had conquered all the known nations. Nebuchadnezzar had everything at his fingertips and everything under his control.

He looked at the great wall that was over 350 feet high and 87 feet thick. He viewed the 250 watchtowers on the wall and admired the hanging gardens—a wonder of the world—overshadowing the city some 300 feet in the air. He surveyed the 53 temples and the 180 altars dedicated to the heathen god, Ishtar,[1] and then said, "Is not this great Babylon, that I have built for a royal dwelling by my mighty power and for the honor of my majesty?" (Dan. 4:30).

It is at this point that God withdrew His blessings. Nebuchadnezzar forgot that every good gift comes from God. The result was a severe case of madness. "He was driven from men and ate grass like oxen; his body was wet with the dew of heaven till his hair had grown like eagles' feathers and his nails like birds' claws" (Dan. 4:33).

Although the consequences may not be so drastic in our own lives, we are suffering from the same kind of selfishness as Nebuchadnezzar. And our selfishness has brought us everything from high blood pressure and urban decay to the absence of community and integrity in relationships.

In a practical sense, we experience the results of selfishness in the erosion of quality in almost every area of life, work, and service. As a result of the me-first worldview, for instance, drastic measures are now needed to deal with automobiles and appliances in constant need of repair. Many items seem to break down as soon as their warranties expire. We cope constantly with fluctuation of supply and demand that intermittently attacks the dollar and a bizarre kind of inflation. Prices seem to keep rising even though consumer demand often slumps. Unemployment plagues us as we move from an industrial society to a service society. Billions of dollars are doled out to people on welfare, and the influx of foreign-made clothing and goods often forces American enterprises to go bankrupt or to close shop.

Somewhere along the line we have forgotten that we did not build this country solely with our own hands. Whatever we have accomplished in establishing our high level of affluence, we have accomplished because we were founded on the knowledge that every good gift comes from God and is to be used to its most productive form.

We keep our joy when we use God's gifts to the best advantage for His glory, the ministry to others, and our own highest good.

APPROPRIATE USE OF GOD'S GIFTS YIELDS SPIRITUAL BENEFITS

In Ecclesiastes 3:12, The Teacher made it clear that the gifts of God properly appropriated result in happiness, goodness, prosperity, and satisfaction.

Once we establish a time philosophy on the premise that every good gift comes from God and then utilize our time to appropriate these gifts according to God's Word, the results are astounding.

This is what the psalmist was talking about when he said,

"Delight yourself also in the LORD, / And He shall give you the desires of your heart" (Ps. 37:4).

This is the formula propounded by Proverbs 3:9,10, "Honor the LORD with your possessions, / And with the firstfruits of all your increase; / So your barns will be filled with plenty, / And your vats will overflow with new wine."

This is Christ's message to His disciples in Luke 6:38, "Give, and it will be given to you: good measure, pressed down, shaken together, and running over will be put into your bosom. For with the same measure that you use, it will be measured back to you."

The process is not only to view time as a gift of God, but to schedule the appropriate sharing and utilization of all our resources as a sacrifice of praise (see Heb. 13:15,16).

In this regard the Bible talks about four levels of giving:

1. *Proportionate Giving:* Deuteronomy 16:17 tells us to give as we are able, which means we are to give in keeping with our respective fiscal capabilities. As the Scripture says, "Every man shall give as he is able, according to the blessing of the LORD your God which He has given you."

2. *Systematic Giving:* First Corinthians 16:2 reminds us to give each Lord's Day in a regular fashion. As Paul stated, "On the first day of the week let each one of you lay something aside, storing up as he may prosper, that there be no collections when I come." This level of giving involves planning and budgeting for the Lord's work in the same way that we plan and budget to meet our own needs.

3. *Sacrificial Giving:* Second Corinthians 9:7 encourages us to give as we purpose in our hearts with a cheerful attitude, and Matthew 10 expresses the importance of freely giving as we freely receive. In these two instances our giving is to be over and above what is required in mere tithing. The joy of giving is the result of sharing abundantly in a way that helps others that are less fortunate.

4. *Expectant Giving:* Malachi 3:10 assures us we can expect a blessing we cannot contain, and Christ promised that our investment in the kingdom will bring us a return one hundred times as much in this present age "and in the age to come, eternal life" (Mark 10:30). In this regard, tithing is the norm in that it is the way God has chosen to establish His kingdom through the agency of the church. However, it is not giving for the sake of giving. Rather, it is the consecration of ourselves in the expectancy that the relationship with the Father will produce reciprocal blessings from His boundless resources. In this way we prosper in order to share that prosperity for the teaching, preaching, and practice of the gospel throughout the world. This is the mission of the church financed by believers who tithe relying upon the faithfulness of the Father.

Using God's resources is directly connected to our scheduling, and the way we schedule determines the level of our joy. When we fail to use God's gifts appropriately, we run the risk of losing our sense of peace and contentment.

This was the case of a man who had a profound influence on my life and ministry. He was a dynamic speaker and a splendid musician. He was a family man who had everything going for him in every way.

Then his priorities changed. He decided he wanted to become a millionaire, and he forgot that the gifts God had given him were to be used for the highest good.

He started living selfishly, and the first thing that changed was his time schedule. No longer did he give his ministry priority; rather, he became interested in business ventures and get-rich-quick schemes. No longer did he spend quality time with his wife and family; rather, he frequently scheduled luncheon appointments, lounge meetings, and late night dinners with business prospects and other people who could "do him good."

What a tragedy to watch this man of God become a man controlled by the world. He made his million dollars, but it cost him not only his ministry, but his wife, his family and, ultimately, his self-respect.

It didn't have to be that way. He had the capacity to be a millionaire without paying such a terrible price. His problem was that he stopped treasuring his time. Instead of appropriating God's gift in God's way, he took matters into his own hands and, like Nebuchadnezzar, decided that he had built his own Babylon.

Making a million dollars isn't the issue, but using God's gifts appropriately to achieve spiritual results is. We succeed when we forget success and start doing what brings success—namely, appropriating God's gifts in the way that yields spiritual benefits.

ASSUME ACCOUNTABILITY

A biblical philosophy of time demands a sense of accountability. This is what The Teacher meant when he explained that everything God has done for us is so that we will revere Him (see Eccles. 3:14). Verses 1 through 8 of Ecclesiastes 3 give us insight into the importance of this accountability, for there is

> A time to be born,
>   And a time to die;
> A time to plant,
>   And a time to pluck what is planted;
> A time to kill,
>   And a time to heal;
> A time to break down,
>   And a time to build up;
> A time to weep,
>   And a time to laugh;
> A time to mourn,
>   And a time to dance;

A time to cast away stones,
  And a time to gather stones;
A time to embrace,
  And a time to refrain from embracing;
A time to gain,
  And a time to lose;
A time to keep,
  And a time to throw away;
A time to tear,
  And a time to sew;
A time to keep silence,
  And a time to speak;
A time to love,
  And a time to hate;
A time for war,
  And a time of peace.

This is what Paul was driving at in 1 Corinthians 4:1,2 when he stated emphatically, "Let a man so consider us, as servants of Christ and stewards of the mysteries of God. Moreover it is required in stewards that one be found faithful." We are accountable to God to use our resources as persons who have been trusted with "the mysteries of God."

Paul brought the matter into sharp focus when he told the Corinthians, "He who sows sparingly will also reap sparingly, and he who sows bountifully will also reap bountifully" (2 Cor. 9:6). The end result is that "you are enriched in everything for all liberality, which causes thanksgiving through us to God" (2 Cor. 9:11).

THE BOTTOM LINE

The bottom line is we must use our time in such a way that will make the biblical philosophy work.

I remember the Bullock family sitting as a group in my office. The husband and wife were on the verge of divorce.

He was a design consultant who had done extremely well, but he worked long hours and was away from home a lot. His absence put an extra burden on his wife, who had the full responsibility for rearing a teenage girl, a grammar-school son, and a two-year-old baby. In the wife's words, "I have had it. I can no longer cope with the problems of three children and cover for an absentee father. He is just never around when I need him."

His side of the story was, "We have to eat. I have spent a lifetime building this business. It is just now paying off. I'm not about to neglect it, regardless of what she says."

The daughter made her pitch by saying, "Dad is never around to see my softball games or do anything with me. He comes in late and leaves early. On the weekends he plays golf or has to go to the office. It's like we don't even have a father."

It took a while, but we started by charting the biblical philosophy of time and then working on a schedule that could relieve the situation and provide more togetherness.

In the process, a methodology emerged to treasure time and make the moments count.

First, *they analyzed their regular use of time*. They explored such questions as: (1) Just exactly how is each family member engaged? (2) What time is the family at home, and how is that time used? (3) Is it really necessary for the husband to spend all that time at the office? (4) Does the daughter really have to be on the go that much? (5) Can the wife rearrange some things and meet her husband in town for lunch and, on occasion, travel with him?

It soon became apparent that while the schedules were tight, more time was available than they thought.

Second, *they made scheduling a family affair*. Every weekend a family council was held, and the schedules for the coming week were synchronized. During this time the father was able to arrange his week to accommodate the daughter's game schedules more often than he had thought possible. Also, by planning far enough in advance for such things as family outings, dinners out together, husband-wife dates, and goofing-off time with his son, family priorities were put on par with many of the business demands.

Third, *the day was started with a family devotion.* This was tough because it meant beginning breakfast thirty minutes earlier so the family could eat with the father, who left early to miss the morning traffic jams.

It took some doing, but after a while each person adjusted. The agenda called for eating breakfast and then sharing ten to fifteen minutes of an appropriate Bible reading, short personal observations, testimonies, requests for prayer, and a final prayer together for God's blessings during the day.

Fourth, *spiritual vitamins were given consistent priority.* Sometimes we call them the grooves of grace, but if we are to grow as Christians, it is important that these seven basic spiritual vitamins be considered: (1) *study* of the Word, formally and informally; (2) *prayer,* corporate and personal; (3) *giving,* financially and benevolently; (4) *witnessing,* in word and in deed; (5) *fellowship* with others in spiritual interaction; (6) *service,* in the church and for the needs of others; and (7) *growth,* through Christian education, indepth spiritual experiences, and regular attendance at public worship.

Obviously such scheduling was tricky, but the Bullock family sorted out the Sunday school classes they could attend; found a sharing group to meet with once a month; accepted a place of service in ushering and welcoming; worked out a time to invite their close friends and neighbors to the sharing group as an opportunity to witness; made personal prayer, study, and private moments an individualized affair in keeping with their own unique personalities and time allowances.

The family members learned to treasure their time, and in the words of the husband, "It's like we have a brand-new lease on life. Sometimes the whole system breaks down and we have to regroup, but we have found a method that works for us."

So, here it is. We treasure our time when we (1) *Analyze:* Check out our committed time and our wasted time, and then decide how much time we really have to use—to treasure for its highest good; (2) *Synchronize:* Share the family priorities and then decide what events are necessary, determine when these events can be attended, and make scheduling in advance an important priority; (3) *Spiritualize:* Make devotional time a regular part of daily activities; (4) *Programize:* Take the seven spiritual vitamins consistently to live in the grooves of grace in the church and the home; and (5) *Personalize:* Set aside individual time for private relaxation and activity.

This is the bottom line. If we want to keep our joy, we must treasure our time with a biblical philosophy that recognizes that every gift comes from God; that the appropriate use of God's gifts yields spiritual benefits; and that we are accountable for the way these gifts are used in our lives.

12 *Stress Point*

The Need for Divine Relationship

PERSONALIZING YOUR PRAYER

Scriptural
Source

Matthew 6:9–13

Joy
Sustainers

Exert a position of power
Expect God's participation
Express petitions in faith
Exercise the promises of God
Energize the reality of eternal life

12

PERSONALIZING YOUR PRAYER

Has it ever occurred to you that the design of prayer in the divine economy is a fantastically puzzling mystery? Why do we need a plan of prayer at all? Is not God almighty and self-sufficient? Could He possibly need any help outside of Himself? Does He need anything that man or any of His creatures can supply?

Why does God want us to pray? Is He not able to effect human redemption without human cooperation in prayer and faith? Why does God not arbitrarily and without reference to any other being or intelligence not proceed to act, to speak, and accomplish His will?[1]

There are no easy answers to such complex questions; yet we do know that while Jesus Christ was on earth, one of the most productive dimensions of His teaching was opening up the horizons of prayer. He told us that we "ought always to pray and not lose heart" (Luke 18:1). Because of this strong emphasis on a prayer life, it becomes obvious that prayer has great meaning not only to us but also to God. In fact, the maintenance of our joy is directly proportional to a prayer life that has regular communion and fellowship with God.

Because of this need for communion and fellowship, prayer is God's invitation to us to share in the divine life as revealed to us in Christ and His Word. *It is God's invitation to participate in a full partnership* with Him as we truly become a part of His body, the church, that lives the kind of life that "the gates of Hades shall not prevail against" (Matt. 16:18). It is God's invitation to us to represent Him in living out His kingdom in the world. The apostle Paul said that we are epistles, "known and read by all men" (2 Cor. 3:2).

Christ gave His disciples a model prayer that we now call the Lord's Prayer. He wanted them to personalize prayer in such a way that would give each of them the assurance that the Father was present as sustainer, redeemer, and resource to cope with all of life's happenings.

Thus, we find Christ on a grassy hillside on the Sea of Galilee, and He gave His disciples a universal message applicable to us all. In this message He made this statement,

> In this manner, therefore, pray:
> Our Father in heaven,
> Hallowed be Your name.
> Your kingdom come,
> Your will be done
> On earth as it is in heaven.
> Give us this day our daily bread.
> And forgive us our debts,
> As we forgive our debtors.
> And do not lead us into temptation,
> But deliver us from the evil one.
> For Yours is the kingdom and the
> power and the glory forever.
> Amen (Matt. 6:9–13).

But how do we apply this prayer to our lives in the twentieth century?

PERSONALIZED PRAYER IS POSITIONAL

Our Father in heaven, / Hallowed be Your name.

First, *we personalize our prayer when we claim our rightful position in Christ*. By saying, "Our Father," we automatically indicate that we have a special relationship with God. We do not have to approach Him with fear; rather, we come in the spirit of adoption knowing that we are His children. As Romans 8:16,17 says, "The Spirit Himself bears witness with our spirit that we are children of God, and if children, then heirs—heirs of God and joint heirs with Christ, if indeed we suffer with Him, that we may also be glorified together."

Further, Paul described the meaning of our position by saying,

> But when the fullness of the time had come, God sent forth His Son, born of a woman, born under the law, to redeem those who were under the law, that we might receive the adoption as sons. And because you are sons, God has sent forth the Spirit of His Son into our hearts, crying out, "Abba, Father!" Therefore you are no longer a slave but a son, and if a son, then an heir of God through Christ (Gal. 4:4–7).

Perhaps the number one difficulty of many believers today is accepting the position of heirship. We talk a lot about the importance of receiving healing for past painful experiences which have haunted us with nagging, hurtful memories. As a result, many people persistently seek the Lord to deliver them from these shadowy holds of the past. Certainly, this healing is important, but it can never really happen until we can accept the full meaning of being justified by faith. As children of God, we have a totally clean slate just as if we had never sinned.

The truth of this principle was brought home to me in a very vivid manner during the early seventies. The hippie movement was flourishing, and downtown Atlanta had a ten-block section that was inhabited by over two thousand young people living the hippie lifestyle.

On the one hand, this community was a tourist novelty. On the other hand, it was a tragic human drama. Drugs were rampant; young people were obsessed with pornography and sexual license; as many as twenty and thirty persons were living in one-room apartments with all the accompanying squalor and filth; in addition, it posed a problem of high crime, prostitution, and general disturbance.

In an effort to reach people strung out on drugs, I became a part of a counseling program. The process involved going among the hippies and trying to persuade drug users to come to the center for treatment and counseling. We had some success, and many drug-free young people returned to society.

One day I was walking through an alley making my rounds, and I saw a young man sitting among some garbage cans trying to give himself a fix. In a cold sweat and shaking all over, he had some problems inserting the needle into a vein.

Spotting me, he called out and asked me to help him make the injection. My first impulse was to come to his aid and enable him to be relieved. Then my own value system kicked in, and I couldn't conscientiously cooperate.

Suddenly, I thought about the first miracle of the disciples after Pentecost. On the spur of the moment I went to him and said, "I can't help you with the injection, but I have something that will help you." At this point I remembered Peter's words to the man who had been lame since birth. Each day he begged at the temple gate in Jerusalem. Peter said to him, "Silver and gold I do not have, but what I do have I give you: In the name of Jesus Christ of Nazareth, rise up and walk" (Acts 3:6).

I then told the young man that I wanted to help him and pray for him. After some discussion he consented. I prayed, and miraculously, he experienced calmness and clarity of thought. This enabled me to reason with him and persuade him to come with me to the counseling center.

Through medical treatment, counseling, and eventual involvement in our church, he turned his life around. It was a long period of ups and downs, and his most difficult problem was accepting his new position in Christ as a totally new creation.

Somehow he caught on to the essential message of Matthew 16:19—that he had the keys to the kingdom and had to use those keys to be an overcomer. He literally bound his old life and loosed his new one. He bound his sordid habits and loosed his new sense of responsibility. He bound his shameful past and loosed his renewed position in Jesus Christ.

Finally, he was able to sustain a job, and he began to grow spiritually into emotional wholeness. After a couple of years he returned to his home in Kentucky to go back to college. A year later, I received a Christmas card that had a note scrawled as follows:

> Do you remember the boy you found in the alley? I just wanted you to know that all is well, and I have entered the ministry. In fact I am serving as the interim pastor of a small community church while I go to school and they find a full-time pastor. Thank you for all you helped me become in Christ.

It all starts out with the position—"Our Father in heaven, / Hallowed be Your name."

PERSONALIZED PRAYER IS PARTICIPATIVE

Your kingdom come, / Your will be done / On earth as it is in heaven.

Second, *we personalize our prayer when we participate in God's work on the earth.* When Christ said to pray "Your kingdom come, /

Your will be done," He was saying that through prayer God participates in our lives in the development and completion of His kingdom.

Christ was talking about this in Luke 17:21 when He told the Pharisees and lawyers that the kingdom is within. This is what He meant in Matthew 12:50 when He exclaimed that whoever does the will of His Father would be related to Him in the same way as a brother, mother, or sister. This is what He called for in John 13:15 when He said, "I have given you an example, that you should do as I have done to you." This is what Paul reinforced when he wrote to the Romans and gave the message that those "whom He foreknew, He also predestined to be conformed to the image of His Son" (Rom. 8:29).

No wonder Billheimer states that God's only handmaiden is the church, "and the nations of the world are but puppets manipulated by God for the purposes of His church (Acts 17:26). Creation has no other aim. History has no other goal."[2] It is clear that God participates.

It is no wonder that Billheimer would then say, "Prayer is where the action is," and E. M. Bounds would add that "God shakes the world by prayer."[3]

Does personalized prayer work in a practical sense? In answer, I offer one woman's experience related in the following letter:

Several years ago I lost an infant son. At that time I did not know Jesus. For years I questioned, yelled, and screamed at God.

I could not express my grief at the time as everyone else was falling apart. Five years after we moved to Colorado my marriage dissolved. . . .

I went hither and yon and finally found Jesus Christ as Lord and Savior. Still questioning my son's death I asked, "Why?"

and was shown all the steps leading to my salvation and baptism in the Holy Spirit.

I then had to leave my parents whose presence would have hindered my knowing the Lord. I prayed for days afterward asking God to help me. I thought I had really loved and trusted Him, but I came to realize I truly did not. I was still steeped in superstition.

The fear of a punishing God is now diminishing. My love for Him is becoming real and not just a service. My trusting in His will is increasing daily.

Since that time my marriage has been restored and taken on a new dimension. We are living each day, praising God for each other, working together, sharing and trying to be good stewards of our time to share the workload at home, church and ministering to others as never before.

We realize we just don't have the time to be inhibited, and we cannot be afraid to step out, for the time is short.

This woman personalized her prayer and found it to be a living fact—personalized prayer is participative because God participates with us when we pray.

PERSONALIZED PRAYER IS PETITIONAL

Give us this day our daily bread. / And forgive us our debts, / As we forgive our debtors.

Third, *we personalize our prayer when we petition God for all our needs and become transparent before Him in our relationship with others.*

In giving us the model prayer, Christ pointed out in these verses that God wants to hear from us and then wants to help us make the necessary adjustments in our personal lives to have real joy.

It is one thing to have everything we need, and yet another to be in right relationship with others to enjoy what we have. It is easier to be happy if we are married to persons we love, but if we never see each other and live as prisoners of loneliness, bitterness, anger, rage, animosity, and malice, what difference does love make? Our petitions are to be not only for the tangibles of life but for the inner dimensions that make or break us in pursuit of the joy of Christian living.

Perhaps this truth is best illustrated by the case of the music minister of a large church who, in a moment of weakness, had an affair with the organist and then the two of them moved to Pennsylvania to live happily ever after. A church was devastated; two homes were broken; a community was embarrassed; children were left puzzled, bewildered, and bitter.

Then the idyllic became erratic, and the erratic became conflict. Both the music minister and the organist realized the seriousness of their behavior and wanted to return to their families.

Two days before Christmas a knock came on my office door. Since it was evening, I was alone, and upon opening the door, I found the man asking for an opportunity to talk. Although I had never seen him before, I invited him in and listened to his story.

He was on his way back home to try a reconciliation with his wife, and he had spotted our church from the highway. Filled with guilt and fear, he needed some reinforcement and took a chance to find someone in the church who would listen. After we talked, he asked me to call his wife.

Her responses were hostile, bitter, and remorseful, and I understood the reasons for her deep hurt and even greater humiliation. Yet at that moment it was as though the Lord inspired me to share the part of the model prayer about asking for forgiveness as we forgive. I recited it to her and asked what it meant to her.

Somehow the Holy Spirit spoke to her heart. The Word touched her. In the course of our conversation, she agreed to seek help and explore the possibilities of reconciliation with her husband.

A month later I received a call from this man and his wife. The miracle of forgiveness was at work. He had been home for two days. The appropriate restitution had been made to the church and the organist's family. Things were looking up.

It wasn't all roses, but from that start the relationship was strengthened. Ultimately, a ministry was restored, and a victory in the power of Christ was recorded.

The wife wrote to me and said,

> I have never thought of the importance of that one phrase in the Lord's Prayer before. I have learned the meaning of forgiveness the hard way. In some respects I can truly identify with the crucifixion of Christ, but then, I remember, if Christ died to forgive me, how much more should I forgive the one person I love the most. Each day we repeat the Lord's Prayer together and petition God for the spirit of forgiveness in every area of our relationship.

This is the presence of true joy—overcoming the bitterness of the hard blows in life to experience the blessings of the forgiving attitudes found in Jesus Christ.

PERSONALIZED PRAYER IS PRESERVATIVE

And do not lead us into temptation, / But deliver us from the evil one.

Fourth, *we personalize our prayer when we trust God to preserve us in times of stress*.

It would be wonderful if we were all immune to or exempt from trouble. To be sure, this is not the case, and we all go through bad times. The point of prayer is that we tap into the preserving power of God to see us through.

Temptation as it is used in this sense is more than the allurement and seduction to evil or wrongdoing. In fact, most scholars believe the best translation is "trial" or "testing."

Every day *we are tested in the natural world* with volcanoes, earthquakes, fires, floods, pestilences, accidents, disease, and death.

Every day *we are tested in the intellectual world* with faulty human judgments colored by unfair and manipulative treatment. Often we are victimized by bias, proudful logic, and lustful intentions. In this regard we reflect our times with such movies as *9 to 5.* Further, we crowd our courtrooms with endless court cases of embezzlement, fraud, and unfair business practices.

Every day *we are tested in the emotional world* by grief, anxiety, hostility, and hatred. Destructive attitudes shrink our spirits. Envy stings us; hate embitters us; greed eats away at us; confidences are betrayed; the rich step on the poor; the poor attempt to dethrone the rich. The result is evident in overcrowded prisons, hospitals, and mental institutions that mark a sense of national emotional upheaval.

Every day *we are tested in the spiritual world.* The Bible describes life as an inward battle (see Rom. 7:22,23); an invisible battle (see Eph. 6:12); a spiritual battle (see 2 Cor. 10:4); a faith battle (see 1 Tim. 6:12); and a priority battle (see 2 Tim. 2:4). Consequently, there are times when we feel as if we are out of harmony with God. Evil tendencies seem to dominate our moods. We struggle with the drag of Romans 7:21, "I find then a law, that evil is present with me, the one who wills to do good."

It is at this point that prayer becomes both a restorer and a retainer of joy. As we pray, we depend on God to lead us in a spiritual walk that copes with and overcomes evil wherever it crosses our path.

This is what Paul was talking about when he closed Romans 7 by saying, "I thank God—through Jesus Christ our Lord!" (v. 25). Then he opened up Romans 8 with a whole new outlook on life: "There is therefore now no condemnation to those who are in Christ Jesus. . . . For the law of the Spirit of life in Christ Jesus has made me free from the law of sin and death" (Rom. 8:1,2).

Having established this preservation power in his life, Paul gave us the clue to overcoming the temptations of life through his own experience in the Roman prison. In his second letter to Timothy, written as a prisoner chained to a Roman guard, he shared his heart by saying:

> For I am already being poured out as a drink offering, and the time of my departure is at hand. I have fought the good fight, I have finished the race, I have kept the faith. Finally, there is laid up for me the crown of righteousness, which the Lord, the righteous Judge, will give to me on that Day, and not to me only but also to all who have loved His appearing (2 Tim. 4:6–8).

.PERSONALIZED PRAYER IS PROJECTIVE

For Yours is the kingdom and the power and the glory forever. Amen.

Finally, *we personalize our prayer when we project the full meaning of life as having eternal significance.*

Too often we fail to understand the eternality of existence as people who believe in God. Christ told us not to let our hearts be troubled because He has prepared an eternal existence for us in complete fellowship with Him (John 14:1–4).

Surrounded as we are by the secularistic humanism of our day, we may find it difficult to project ourselves into the future that God has planned for us.

Nonetheless we know that death is inevitable. It affects us all directly and indirectly. Someone close to us may die, and we feel the effect very keenly. Someone dear to us suffers for a prolonged period of time, and we stand by in a state of frustrated helplessness. Someone distant to us dies, yet we are involved. We pay our last respects. We spend time with the grieving family and friends.

In the midst of this, however, the Bible tells us that life and death are not isolated events; they are commensurate. As we live, we die; as we die, we live. In the biblical view, life on earth is temporary. It is depicted as a shadow (see 1 Chron. 29:15), a weaver's shuttle (see Job 7:6), a runner (see Job 9:25), a handbreath (see Ps. 39:5), and a vapor (see James 4:14). The Bible also makes it clear that real life is eternal life. In this sense, death is timeless life. For the believer, it is to be greatly desired (see Num. 23:10). It is not to be feared (see Ps. 23:4) because it is precious (see Ps. 116:15), hopeful (see Prov. 14:32), and triumphant in the resurrection of Christ (see 1 Cor. 15:55–57). It is a blessing (see Rev. 14:13) that is divine (see Rom. 14:8) and advantageous (see Phil. 1:21).

Through prayer, we touch the heart of a God who cares, comforts, sustains, and strengthens. Our joy is maintained because we know that real life is ultimately eternal life.

This knowledge gives us the ability to deal with whatever comes our way in a positive manner. We believe in miracles, but we also believe in maintenance faith. Hebrews 11:32–35a gives a picture of a miracle faith that even accomplished the resurrection of dead children, but verses 35b–40 depict a maintenance faith in the midst of suffering that produced a divine quality of life.

Our responsibility is to trust and believe God for the miracles and at the same time to develop the inner resiliency to make suffering a ministry of maintenance faith until either the miracle of healing or the miracle of death occurs.

This was the case of Jim, who suffered a massive stroke that forced him to be bedridden for nine years. Visiting him during that time was an experience of joy, because he had developed the inner strength that prepared him for whatever came first— healing or death. "I am in God's hands," he said. "If necessary,

I will minister through suffering to encourage others to meet their circumstances with faith." At his death there was an evident spirit of celebration and peace. It was as though Jim had achieved his highest goal—to be with Christ. He was a man with a maintenance faith as exemplified in Hebrews 11:32–40.

In effect we maintain a joy that projects the reality of eternal existence as demonstrated to us in the resurrection of Jesus Christ.

Here is the path to the fullest meaning of joy—learning to pray in a personalized way.

The Lord's Prayer as we have come to know it is really our own personal prayer, and it becomes a joy sustainer as we exert our positions in Christ, expect His participation in our lives, express our petitions in faith, exercise the promises of His preservation, and energize our outlook by projecting the reality of eternal existence.

With these insights in focus, we know that joy describes a lifestyle of deep inner satisfaction—regardless of the circumstances.

This is the lifestyle that carries us through the difficult days with a song in our hearts.

As God's people we are to sing a song to the Lord . . . to shout for joy . . . to sing a hymn of praise to God . . . to sing His praises from the ends of the earth . . . to sing the song of Moses . . . to sing the song of the servant of God . . . to sing the song of the Lamb (see Ps. 33:3; Ps. 40:3; Isa. 42:10; Rev. 15:3).

The question is, "How shall we sing the LORD's song in a strange land?" (Ps. 137:4). How do we keep our joy?

In answer we have shared together a twelve-step plan for living and maintaining a productive life of joy.

1. Accept joy as a spiritual source to meet your inadequacies.
2. Decide to live a life of discipleship in Christ as the fulfillment of the meaning of life.
3. Develop a positive thought process in the peace of Christ to

guard against the invasion of negative thought conditioners.

4. Practice a vitalized vocabulary of faith that reflects the image of Christ and transcends the negative speech patterns of a world in fear.

5. Internalize the new life of self-worth in Christ that strives for the highest ideals and replaces the old life with its distorted self image.

6. Plan your priorities based on the timeless life in Christ that brings balance and stability in a day of ambivalence and confusion.

7. Discipline your desires with a decision to live "hidden in Christ" (see Col. 3:3) as the deterrent to the pressure of perversion.

8. Focus your faith on the person and work of Christ within as the security of strength for the pain of emptiness.

9. Neutralize the negatives of circumstances and situations with an optimistic outlook and personalized code for living based on the Word.

10. Transcend the tragedies of life with a profound trust in the living God of the Bible who works for good and finishes what He starts in the promise of eternal life.

11. Treasure your time as a gift of God to be used for its highest level of productivity.

12. Personalize your prayer as a constant flow of sustaining energy from an ongoing relationship with God—the Father.

NOTES

Chapter 1

1. Paul H. Walker, *Paths of a Pioneer* (Cleveland, Tenn.: Church of God Publishing Co., 1971), p. 313.
2. Gerhard Kittel and Gerhard Friedrich, *Theological Dictionary of the New Testament,* vol. 7 (Grand Rapids, Mich.: Wm. B. Eerdmans Publishing Co., 1971), p. 637.
3. Salynn Boyles, "Sports Lover Jason Garner Fights Lymphoma," *East Cobb Neighbor* [Marietta, Georgia], April 19, 1984.
4. Robert L. Thorndike and Elizabeth Hagin, *Measurement and Evaluation in Psychology and Education,* 2nd ed. (New York: John Wiley & Sons, Inc., 1967), p. 317.
5. Felicia Lee, "Cynical Attitude Harms Health," *USA Today,* October 18, 1984.

Chapter 2

1. David Barrett, *The World Christian Encyclopedia* (London: Oxford University Press, 1982).
2. Bill J. Leonard, "Where Are the Clowns?" *Pulpit Digest,* May–June 1979, p. 3.
3. Donald Macleod, "A Steady Fact in Unsteady Times," *Pulpit Digest,* January–February 1984, p. 45.
4. Charles Allen, *Life More Abundant* (Old Tappan, N.J.: Revell, 1968), pp. 56–61.

Chapter 5

1. National Institute of Mental Health, *Mental Health, United States 1985.* C. A. Taube and S. A. Barrett, eds. (DHS Pub #[ADM] 85-1378, Washington, D.C. Supp. of DRS., U.S. Government Printing Office, 1985), pp. v, vi.

Chapter 6

1. Tim LaHaye, *The Battle for the Mind* (Old Tappan, N.J.: Revell, 1980), p. 83.
2. Ibid., p. 96.

Chapter 7

1. Eric Liddell, *The Disciplines of the Christian Life* (Nashville, Tenn.: Abingdon Press, 1985), p. 18.
2. Ibid., pp. 29–30.
3. Paul Walker, *The Ministry of Church and Pastor* (Cleveland, Tenn.: Pathway Press, 1976), pp. 29,30.
4. Stan Telchin, *Betrayed* (Grand Rapids, Mich.: Chosen Books, 1981).

Chapter 8

1. Susan Seliger, "Stress: A Sure Prescription," *New Woman,* November 1982, p. 46.
2. Ibid., p. 48.
3. Ibid., p. 50. "Stress Can Be Good for You," *New York,* August 2, 1982.

Chapter 9

1. Susan Seliger, "Stress: A Sure Prescription," p. 47.

Chapter 10

1. Peg Rankin, *Yet Will I Trust Him* (Ventura, Calif.: Regal Books, 1983), p. 54.
2. Paul E. Billheimer, *Don't Waste Your Sorrow* (Minneapolis: Bethany House Publishers, 1977), p. 70.

Chapter 11

1. H. L. Willmington, "Daniel," *Willmington's Guide to the Bible* (Wheaton, Ill.: Tyndale House Publishers, 1985), pp. 231–32.

Chapter 12

1. Paul E. Billheimer, *Destined for the Throne* (Fort Washington, Pa.: Christian Literature Crusade, 1975), p. 43.
2. Ibid., p. 26.
3. Ibid., p. 102.